# Limoges Boxes

## A Complete Guide

# Faye Strumpf

**Photography by Ann Modisette**

Published by

700 East State Street • Iola, WI 54990-0001

Please call or write us for our free catalog of antiques and collectibles publications. To place an order or receive our free catalog, call 800-258-0929. For editorial comment and further information, use our regular business telephone at (715) 445-2214.

Library of Congress Catalog Number: 99-67649
ISBN: 0-87341-837-9
Printed in the United States of America

# Dedication

**This book is dedicated to Evelyn Dullman and Frieda Mintz, my mom and aunt; and to Mary Angela Jordan, Ann Modisette's mom. They were women who appreciated the finest things in life and Limoges, in particular.**

# Acknowledgments

To my family, Hal, Cary and Mike, who went with the ebb and flow of the writing of the book, with special thanks to Mike, for without his computer expertise this would not have been possible and Cary for her thoughtful and constructive help.

To Ann Modisette, friend and companion in photographic adventures.

To Ronnie Gerber whose perspicacity was invaluable to me, and as a friend.

To Sloane Hackwell for her sense of humor and excellent English skills.

To friends and family who have supported me throughout the writing of the book:
Marilyn Ortner, Sari Freedman, Marilyn Fink, Joy Coffey, Muriel Newhauser, Connie and David Luzan, Donald Gerber, Jeanne Millman and Christine and John Sidenfaden. The Dullmans, Eisenberg/Scarboroughs, Weissman/Eisenmans, and Mintz/Kane/Strumpfs.

To Herb Yellin, who acted as a mentor to me during this time of learning.

To Chantal Meslin-Perrier, Director of Musee Adrien Dubouche, for her hospitality in Limoges, her help in checking information and her continued support.

To Dorothy Kamm for her support and allowing the inclusion of some of her collection.

To Liana Paredes Arend, Hillwood Museum, Curator of Western European Art.

The French Alliance in the U.S. and Limoges, France.

Jackie Hershowitz, at the French Consulate in Los Angeles.

Palos Verdes Library staff.

Los Angeles County Museum of Art, Library staff.

Leny Davidson, President of Chamart and niece of Charles Martine for her expertise and graciousness and for allowing us to take pictures of Chamart's extensive collection and use them in the book.

Lucy Zahran of Lucy Zahran & Co., for her kindness and allowing us to photograph items from her collection and use them for the book.

Heather Ryan of Bernardaud for her help and for allowing us to take pictures of their pieces and allowing us to use them in the book.

The staff at Parry Vieille.

Nancy du Tertre at Artoria for her kind assistance on back marks and for allowing us to take pictures of their pieces and use them in the book.

Anny and Jean-Pierre de Chazal of Chanille for allowing us to take pictures of their pieces and use them in the book.

Shirley Dickerson of S & D Collectibles for allowing us to take pictures of their pieces and use them in the book.

Patrick Kelso of DuBarry for allowing us to take pictures of their pieces and use them in the book.

The staff at Halcyon Days.

Chris Christensen for his invaluable information on salt cellars and appraisals.

Debby DuBay of Limoges Antique Shop.

Susan Wolf of Willow Street and Ann Davis of Wallpaper Nook.

Grace Graves, Jan Cruikshank, Nora Travis, Adela Meadows and Haviland Collectors Internationale Foundation.

Elayne Troute of the Perfect Gift.

Mark Chervenka, editor of Antique & Collectors Reproduction News

Finishing Touches Interior Designs.

Jon Brecka, Paul Kennedy and Tracy Schmidt of Krause Publications.

Debbie Glass for editing; Samanta Tashima and Joëlle Petit Adkins at Savoir Faire for translating.

Collectors: Marge Kaplan, Faith Osheroff, Donna Young, Marion Stein, Carole Willis, Debby DuBay, Connie Luzan, Sari Freedman, Corinne Hartman, Marion Adams, Elayne Troute, Marilyn Ortner and others who allowed me to photograph their collections.

Anne and Bob Lohmann of Lohmann's Flowers for their support and use of wonderful flowers.

# Table of Contents

# Foreword

*by Leny Davidson*
*President, Chamart Exclusives, New York*

What a wonderful book this is. We are all indebted to Faye Strumpf for filling one of the voids in the publishing world: the absence of an accurate, clearly written and researched book about the history and technology of Limoges boxes.

Clearly, anyone who spends so much time and effort to create a specialty book like this must love her topic, and Faye's love for our delicious little boxes radiates from every page of this fascinating book.

Faye's book is accurate in terms both of history and porcelain technology; is informative to layman and technician alike, and it is balanced in terms of the highly competitive companies that exist in this microcosm of a market. Perhaps most important, it is genuinely entertaining.

The historical section is exhaustive without being exhausting, covering everything from the early discovery of kaolin in the Limousin region to the gradual creation of the active commercial Limoges industry of the 1990s. The technical section on porcelain fabrication is not only accurate but delightful, with woodcuts interspersed with modern photographs.

Particularly enlightening for those who believe a box is just a box is the section that discusses the categories of boxes, such as etui, carnet de bal, tabatiere, bonbonniere, fantasy, patch box, boite a portrait, freedom box, bibelot, etc. While what had been created centuries ago for very exclusive and specific purposes may now be subsumed in the general mind into the overall category of porcelain boxes, the true Limoges box expert can name each and discuss its precise use.

The best histories are about personalities. In this book we meet grumbling French nobles who were forced by King Louis XV again and again to melt down their silver to pay for his extravagances. To deal with this predicament, they craftily created objects in porcelain, from serving pieces to boxes. Limoges history is populated with historical figures momentarily off their serious pedestals, to be revealed as just people; people with odd and sometimes lovable (and sometimes not) foibles. So further on you will meet Count Heinrich von Bruhl and his 300 suits of clothes, each accompanied by a special snuffbox; and Beau Brummel, whose name is still synonymous with the popinjay slave to fashion, haggling with King George IV over a favorite snuffbox; and more eccentric characters animated less by serious affairs of state than by their love of these lovely little porcelain works of art.

Of particular interest to collectors will be Faye's section on searching for pieces, negotiating with dealers, the difference between the real thing and the clever fake (alas, a reality in all fields of collecting); and backstamps which identify and date Limoges boxes as accurately as hallmarks identify British silver.

What an odd little passion we all share, a passion which has animated so many men and women, past and present. Today's collector of Limoges has a long heritage, if not always a glorious one, at least a fascinating and often quaint one. Faye has restored our unknown predecessors to us, and many of us will be surprised, and perhaps not a little pleased, to find so many kings and queens and noblemen in our family tree of Limoges collectors.

There is magic in Limoges boxes, these tiny, glittering beauties that are at once works of art, witty comments on customs or traditions and mysterious little caches hiding some kind of treasure. This book will make us all better and wiser collectors.

# Introduction

One of life's joys is to behold beautiful things and, in the ideal, to own and cherish them. Limoges boxes are the embodiment of this. These enchanting creations afford one the opportunity to indulge in beauty and sense the past in an intimate way, on a continual basis.

One can look at a Limoges box from many different aspects. What attracts you? The beauty of the porcelain? The grace of the design? The whimsy of the unusual? Is it the echo of a favorite activity? Or the essence of a precious memory? Do you hear the whisper of serenity or feel the anticipation of the mystery inside? Whatever the reason, the keen feeling one gets when looking at Limoges boxes is indescribable and personal. A smile comes to my face just thinking of it. Pleasure has many manifestations; one is the bountiful visual experience you are about to have.

Come with me and look at many things. First, revisit the 18th century when the kaolin for Limoges porcelain was discovered. During this era, the aristocracy reveled in luxury and exuberance. Fantasy and the exotic were pursued to add a piquant aspect to daily experience. Self-indulgence was not anguished over—it was embraced. Life's boundaries were broad and innovations were sought. Whimsy and capriciousness were enticing. Days were spent seeking diversion and excellence.

You will also find included for your enjoyment a brief history of Limoges porcelain, a visit to Limoges and how porcelain is made. You'll peruse a bevy of boxes old and new, glimpse the ritual of snuff taking and other old world obsessions and take a look at fakery. I've included collecting tips, helpful glossaries, guides and source information.

Come. Join me. A visual feast awaits!

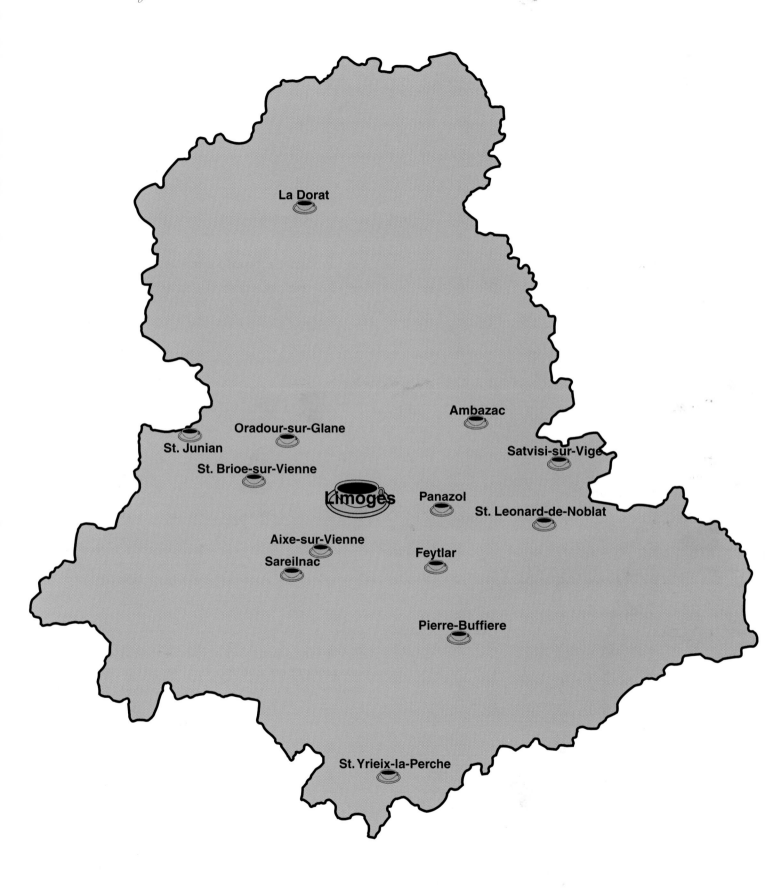

La Dorat

Ambazac

Oradour-sur-Glane

St. Junian

Satvisi-sur-Vige

St. Brioe-sur-Vienne

Limoges

Panazol

St. Leonard-de-Noblat

Aixe-sur-Vienne

Feytlar

Sareilnac

Pierre-Buffiere

St. Yrieix-la-Perche

*Limousin Region of France*

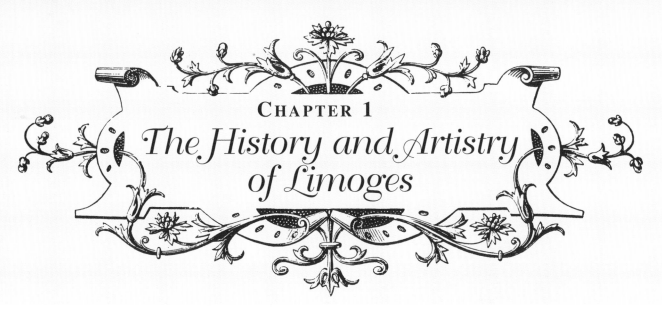

# CHAPTER 1
# The History and Artistry of Limoges

## A Brief History of Limoges

The city of Limoges (pronounced *le-mozh*) has long been a center for the production of fine arts. Although it is now known for porcelain, its art-related history started in the 12th century with champleve enamel work. Boxes and other items were made in Limoges at that time and were exquisitely created in intricate designs in enamel. During that time, Limoges was the finest source of champleve enamel work in Europe, but tastes change, so Limoges artisans started creating painted enamels. These enamels continued and existed concurrently with porcelain. So, the Limoges artisans have been supplying us with luxury items for nearly a thousand years. The tradition of producing fine *objets d' art* continues in the striking Limoges porcelain boxes being made today.

The Roman gods from Limoges' ancient history must have been smiling down when kaolin, the hard white clay which was the basic ingredient for true porcelain, was discovered in the Limousin region. The term for porcelain comes from *porcella-na*, the Italian (and Portuguese) word for the cowrie shell which porcelain is said to resemble in color and texture. There was much confusion about the procedures for making porcelain and what constituted its properties. At the end of the 16th century, it was thought by some that porcelain was made up of a combination containing egg, chalk, shells of sea locusts and other substances. These things were supposedly mixed together and buried for 80 years, with no one knowing the whereabouts except the maker's children and grandchildren. The "finished" porcelain was then uncovered and used to make vases and other wonderful things.

In reality, true porcelain (also referred to as hard paste porcelain) is composed of kaolin, feldspar and quartz. Kaolin, the key ingredient in hard paste porcelain, was discovered in the Limousin region in 1768 in Saint Yrieix La Perche. Limoges already had a *faience* workshop in production in 1736 run by Andre Massie and, by virtue of that, had knowledgeable people available in terms of ceramic manufacturing. Fortuitously, the area had a river that provided the water necessary for porcelain production, and the local forests provided the wood to fire the kilns. The area seemed fated for success.

## The Discovery of Kaolin

The legend of the discovery of kaolin goes somewhat like this: there was a shortage of soap and a woman named Madame Darnet was using the local clay to lift grease stains from her washing and decided to use it as a whitener. Her husband pursued this idea and gave a sample of it to the apothecary, Marc Hilaire Villaris. Villaris identified the white clay as remarkably pure kaolin. It was said by people at the time that the whiteness and beauty of the kaolin was so incredible that you would have gone down on your knees before it. What they had found was, for them, white gold.

In actuality there was a concerted effort to find French kaolin. The chemists at Sevres (the Royal Manufactory)—Macquer, Millot and Hellot—knew about kaolin since they had done laboratory work on Chinese kaolin and also had samples from Augustus of Saxony. Macquer and Millot had made attempts at porcelain making but none of the results were to their liking. They had also gone to different provinces in France to find a source.

The Archbishop of Bordeaux visited Sevres and upon the request of persons there, took current samples of kaolin to his district to find local kaolin. The Archbishop showed this clay to Villaris, an apothecary, who, in his broad search for the source of this substance, showed it to Jean Baptiste Darnet of Saint Yrieix La Perche. Darnet immediately recognized it as the clay his wife was using as a washing substance. Villaris obtained three pounds of the clay which he sent to Sevres. (From this clay, a statuette of a child Bacchus was made, which is preserved at the Sevres Museum to this day.)

Villaris did not instantaneously tell the Sevres chemists where the clay had come from, hoping to have some monetary gain from his involvement. Millot and Macquer were then sent to the area to discover the kaolin's whereabouts. In their attempts to find it, they came upon some clays and were experimenting with them. The Archbishop then called in Villaris. who was not pleased to see their progress. After hesitating until the next day, Villaris offered his assistance. He would meet them on an appointed date at Tiriee (Saint Yrieix La Perche). Villaris chose a house as far as possible from Darnet's and went by a circuitous route to avoid Darnet's house. As quoted in Auscher's *A History and Description of French Porcelain* (pg. 80), Millot and Macquer recounted that "Villaris made us go through all the gardens on the outskirts of town to reach the kaolin…in a little path so dark that it was almost impossible to see."

As they were digging, someone told the owner of the land that something was amiss. After this, Macquer contacted the mayor and indicated his mission was for the King; the mayor then made it possible for kaolin to be forthcoming. About 400 pounds of kaolin passed through the Customs House at Limoges and was transported to Sevres.

From this shipment, objects were made and on St. Thomas Day (Dec. 21, 1769), a cooking pot made from this shipment's kaolin was placed over a heating lamp and the contents were brought to a boil. (The first attempt earlier in the day was not successful.) Macquer received the compliments of the King at Court. Sevres was, therefore, producing soft and hard paste concurrently.

Saint Yrieix La Perche, the actual site of the deposit, lacked the knowledgeable workforce to engage in production, so the kaolin was transported to Limoges. The triumvirate of knowledge, water and materials made Limoges the ideal location. It took the three years, from 1768 to 1771, to accomplish the beginning of production. The first porcelain item made from this clay was, fittingly, a commemorative medallion. The administrator of Limousin, Turgot, had his coat-of-arms inscribed and noted the event. The factory was run by Joseph Massie, son of Andre Massie, in conjunction with the chemist Nicolas Fourniera (alternately spelled Fournerat), with brothers Pierre and Gabriel Grellet.

The discovery of kaolin was a monumental event. It made French porcelain production possible and heralded the beginning of Limoges' legacy as the center of the hard paste porcelain industry in France.

### Initial Limoges Production

In 1771, the factory of Grellet, Massie and Fourneira came under the patronage of Comte d'Artois. The registered mark was C.D., for the Comte d'Artois, since the area was within the confines of his estate. In 1784, the King officially started using the porcelain factory of Grellet, Massie and Fourneira as an affiliate of Sevres. It produced wares and/or raw materials which were subsequently sent to Sevres for finishing and painting. The son of Grellet was the factory director until 1788, being followed by Francois Alluaud. The production of the royal factory continued on until 1792; the King being considered the director until 1796. Its mark was crossed "L"s and a crown, the royal cipher or monogram. It was called "Royal Porcelain" (or *Porcelaine Royale*) and the year of manufacture of an object was indicated by a letter in the center of the crossed "L"s. The works have passed through different owners to the present time.

### Limoges Outstretched

In the beginning, in addition to production in Limoges, raw materials and/or some unfinished products were sent to Sevres, Paris manufacturers, and other locations in France. The quality of the kaolin was so desirable that raw materials were requested by and sent to such distant places as Switzerland, Holland, Denmark and Russia.

Sevres, the official royal factory, had been producing artificial or soft paste porcelain (designated "French Porcelain" or *Porcelaine de France*) which was renowned for its wide range of spectacular colors and superb workmanship. As the royal factory, it had precedence over all other French porcelain manufactories. It was under the protection of King Louis XV and Madame de Pompadour and was therefore supported by the government. Restrictive constraints were placed on the other porcelain manufacturers, for example, in their use of color and gilding in the decoration of their wares.

Royal support of Sevres also meant that money was spent for innovation in production, discovering new colors, design ideas, techniques and various other areas of improvement. Additionally, since this was done under royal aegis, the individuals involved with production were not just potters but the finest craftsmen and artists available, all working to produce porcelain for Madame de Pompadour and the King. With Madame de Pompadour's death in 1764, France lost a great stateswoman and its patroness for the art of porcelain.

## The Paris Connection

With the discovery of kaolin in the Limousin region, factories opened in other locations using their paste or whites, the most important being the numerous hard paste porcelain factories in Paris. They are referred to as "Paris porcelain" or "Old Paris" and produced hard paste porcelain from about 1770 to the first quarter of the 19th century. At this time there were still restrictive codes in effect, although people sought to circumvent or ignore them. One method of protection used by the Paris factories was to seek the favor of a member of the royal family in the hope that the bending or breaking of restrictions would go unpunished. Some Paris porcelain factories produced multicolored and gilded items (in defiance of the edicts). In reaction to the affront, some token confiscations occurred. In 1773, the dissemination of a restrictive order set off protests from Paris factories. In 1776, Sevres formally put forth grievances against the Paris factories, which included offering higher wages and absconding with Serves property. Searches and confiscations followed. The struggle between Sevres and the Paris factories continued until 1787-1788 when they were allowed most of

the freedoms they desired. This was followed by the Revolution.

Truly, if the restrictive orders had been followed, the hard paste porcelain industry in France as we know it today possibly would not have existed. Several of the Paris porcelain factories were protected by royal family members, as follows:

*Rue Thiroux*: Under the protection of Queen Marie Antoinette, the products were known as *Porcelaine de la Reine*.

*Clignancourt*: Under the protection of Comte de Provence, Louis Stanislas Xavier, brother of Louis XVI and future Louis XVIII.

*Faubourg Saint Denis*: Under the protection of Charles Philippe, Comte d'Artois, Louis XVI's youngest brother and the future Charles X.

*Rue de Bondy*: Under the protection of Duc d'Angouleme, Comte d'Artois' eldest son, who was six years old(!) when he assumed the patronage.

Other Paris porcelain companies existing after 1770: *La Courtille, Gros Caillou, Rue du Petit Carrousel, Rue de Reuilly, Pont aux Choux, Barriere de Reuilly, Rue Amelot, Petite Rue Saint Gilles, Rue de Crussol, Rue de Charonne, Rue de la Roquette, Palais Royal, Rue Popincourt* and *Rue Fontaine au Roi*. The majority of these concerns bought their paste or "whites" in Limoges.

In the years after 1820, conditions were not conducive to Paris porcelain purveyors and most of them migrated to Limoges. Limoges was now the major center for French porcelain.

## Families of Renown

In addition to Grellet and company, there were local land-owning families, Alluaud and Pouyat, who produced incredible work. The Pouyat family engaged in producing exceptional wares, as evidenced in *The National Museum Adrien Dubouche: Limoges*. Jean Pouyat was famous for his white work; his "Rice Service" is an example of his fine openwork pieces. The Pouyat family continued manufacturing until 1932.

The Baignol and Tharaud families were highly respected manufacturers in the early 19th century. Etienne Baignol was an excellent worker in porcelain. He worked at Sevres and had an *atelier* in La Seynie and subsequently moved to Limoges. His work was characterized by high quality, refinement, elegance and variety.

## Limoges Porcelain and the American Market: Haviland

Fine china has always been cherished; Limoges, in addition to being progenitor of

Limoges boxes, is home to Haviland China. Highly coveted by the American market, Haviland was the china of choice of numerous presidents (Lincoln, Grant, Arthur, Hayes, Cleveland and McKinley). They were following in the social footsteps of George Washington, who had purchased French porcelain for his table. Included in his serving pieces was a Limoges porcelain casserole, with the Comte d'Artois mark. French porcelain set the standard for fine china.

Haviland China first began operations in Limoges in 1842 and continues to be operational to this day. In 1836, the Havilands, from their headquarters in New York, were engaged in the importing of English pottery and decided to add French porcelain to their product line. Since American and European tastes in products differed, a decision was made to locate an American branch in France. The porcelain production was then adapted for U.S. tastes. In 1846, David Haviland started a factory in Limoges. The Haviland name has encompassed different branches of the family over the years. (Nora Travis' book is a good source on this.) In 1876, the Haviland Co. instituted the use of manufacturer's marks on its wares. Most of the other Limoges manufacturers did, too. Prior to 1876, marking had not been consistent.

Throughout the years, Haviland has received numerous awards, the first in 1853 at the International Crystal Palace Exhibition in New York. The Haviland name continues to remain associated with excellence and keeps in tune with the design and art fields. At the International Exposition of Decorative Arts and Industrial Modernism in 1925 in Paris, which brought us the term "Art Deco," some wonderful Haviland pieces were shown, including: Jean Dufy's award-winning Chateaux de France; Edouard Marcel Sandoz's unusual designs; and the art on porcelain of Susan(ne) Lalique, wife of Paul Haviland and daughter of Rene Lalique. Artistic innovation continues in Haviland China with the use of artists such as Kandinsky and Cocteau.

## Hand-painting Flourishes

Another chapter in the saga of Limoges porcelain took place starting in the late-1800s and continuing until the early 1900s. At this time, china painting as a hobby and business flourished in the United States. Haviland and most of the other Limoges factories exported undecorated wares to the American market. Included in the category of recipients of the wares was Pickard. His early studio work is now highly desirable. (He at one point wanted to buy a factory in Limoges.)

In France, there was some parallel in terms of hand painting porcelain. There is a tradition of using independent home decorators; a person who does this in France was referred to as a *chambrelan* (in Germany, the person was called a *hausmaler*). Pieces decorated both in France and America at that time are available on the secondary market. Proponents of china painting often preferred Limoges porcelain over other European or Oriental wares.

As Haviland served as the initial conduit of tablewares into the United States, another man served as the importer of the first Limoges hinged boxes. In the mid-1950s, Charles Martine started importing covered boxes in addition to other Limoges items. In the mid-1960s, the company imported the first hinged boxes into the United States.

## Moving to the Present

It has been almost two thousand years since the Limoges area was used as a Roman encampment and 200 years since the community of Limoges came into existence. In the ensuing two centuries, about 70 entrepreneurs have been involved in the porcelain industry. Production of Limoges porcelain manufacturers and American purchasing habits have reflected the changes in the world, with reduction in production in times of strife and war, and increases with stability and prosperity. Products have also changed and reflected the changes in the tastes of society. French law has been enacted designating that only items made in Limoges or the area can say "Limoges."

Having progressed through time, porcelain production continues to echo the desires and fashions of the affluent. We have seen the starkness of Modernism, with its sleek and unusual lines,

**Myth: Limoges is a factory in the town of Limoges.**
*Fact: Limoges is both a city and a region in France. When a piece is marked "made in Limoges," it could be made in the city of Limoges or within the region, which contains other cities.*

**Myth: Limoges is one factory.**
*Fact: In reality, Limoges porcelain is made by various factories, the number of which varies depending on the world economy and the demand for porcelain. In recent years there have been about 40 factories. In addition to the factories, there is the issue of who does the hand-painting. Hand-painting on Limoges boxes is done both by factory painters or independent painters. The independent painters are called* chambrelans, *home based painters.*

**Myth: Limoges is a quaint village or quiet remote place.**
*Fact: Limoges is an industrial city mixed with some lovely sights.*

reflected in the patterns and shapes of china. The 1980s and 1990s have shown a return to a warm and romantic feeling. We now want to surround ourselves with comfort, beauty and the finer things in life. Utility and beauty are combined. We enswathe ourselves in soft textures and buy porcelain and other refinements.

In 1976, the U.S. government designated hand-painted porcelain as a fine art. In keeping with this concept, hand-painted Limoges boxes are miniature pieces of fine art. Thoughts come full circle as this is the same idea about art that Fredrick the Great held in the 18th century.

The United States now supports the superlative products of Haviland, Bernardaud, Raynaud and Goldsmith-Corot. Bernardaud, the largest porcelain manufacturer in France, has opened a boutique on Park Avenue in New York City. In the 1980s, it purchased Ancienne Manufacture Royale and added archival designs, from the 18th century collection of Comte d'Artois. According to Heather Ryan, Bernardaud's U.S. Marketing Director, Bernardaud (in conjunction with the French government) is in the process of creating a living, working Limoges porcelain museum to be located in Limoges on the Bernardaud premises. In addi-

tion, companies such as Baccarat, Faberge and Hermes are using Limoges porcelain manufacturers for their product lines. Also, the Comite Colbert, an association of luxury companies such as Louis Vuitton, Daum and Chanel, includes in its roster various Limoges porcelain manufacturers. (This association is named after Jean Baptiste Colbert, 1619-1683, who was instrumental in promoting French artistic influence.)

In an interesting twist, Halcyon Days (enamel boxes) was said to be producing a *bonbonniere* series using Limoges porcelain bodies and enamel lids. Further checking showed that this was not the case. Recently, Limoges boxes and royalty came together again with Prince Charles, in the commissioning of boxes for charity. So the connection between wonderful, unique porcelain boxes and royalty continues. With Limoges boxes, we now have the joy of the individually hand-painted porcelain that we can hold and cherish! We continue to be the lucky recipients of the search for excellence in porcelain.

As of December 1995, there were about 40 factories working in Limoges. Limoges continues to be synonymous with fine porcelain and is now sold in Italy, Switzerland, England, Scotland, Wales,

*The Adrien Dubouche Museum.*

Belgium, the Netherlands, Luxembourg, Andorra, Germany, Portugal, Spain, Japan, China, Singapore, the Middle East, Australia, New Zealand, Canada and the United States.

As of 1999, the Adrien Dubouche Museum is planning to be coming out with a comprehensive book related to back marks; it should be available around the year 2001.

## A Visit to Limoges

The city of Limoges is located in central France, about 250 miles southwest of Paris, in the Limousin region. In the past, it was home to the Celtic Limovices tribe; at one point in its history, it was a Roman city called Augustoritum. Limoges' location was significant, as it was on a pilgrimage route and was at the crossroads of Roman trade routes.

Presently, Limoges is a city of contradictions. It is a small central old town steeped in history and yet, at the same time, a large industrial city. You could conceive of Limoges as a treasure hunt and seek out the "treasures." Its greatest treasure is the Adrien Dubouche Museum, which is housed in an impressive building built in the 1800s. The outside is graced with magnificent architectural features which suggest the delights you are about to experience. The museum's bounty includes the largest collection of Limoges porcelain in the world. The Museum contains about 11,000 items of ceramic and glassware ranging from ancient Greek to modern manufacture. (There is a wonderful book available about the museum entitled *The National Museum Adrien Dubouche*.)

Another of Limoges' treasures is the visual *carte*. The city's architecture is quite diverse. The building styles include, among others, Medieval, Renaissance, Art Nouveau and industrial contemporary architecture.

The city has a number of venerable sites. The most impressive being its Gothic cathedral, Saint Etienne, which was built on a location used since the 3rd century for a series of churches. Behind the cathedral is the Municipal Museum, located in the Bishop's Palace. Displayed there are Limoges enamels from the Middle Ages on and some works by Pierre Auguste Renoir, native of Limoges, who began his artistic career as a porcelain decorator in Paris. Also displayed are archaeological, mineral and lapidary objects. Below Bishop's Palace lies a monument which is called the "Lovers." As the tale goes, the young couple was going on a pilgrimage, the wife died and the husband continued the pilgrimage in her memory. On returning to Limoges, he died and their souls were then reunited. Surrounding the cathedral is Limoges' botanical gardens.

Located in an area formerly the center for the town's butchers and facing a bricked and timbered building on Rue de Canal, is the church of St. Aurelian. The church was built in 1475 (denoted by a plaque on the face of the church), on the location previously used in the 5th century. The stone carvings evoke bygone times.

Balustraded steps lead to the area of St. Martial's crypt. It is said that his place of burial formed the nexus of the town. Another architectural sight is Limoges' Art Deco train station,

*Saint Etienne, Gothic cathedral. Behind the cathedral is the Bishop's Palace, which houses the Municipal Museum (Musee Municipal de L'Eveche).*

*Medieval bridge*

St. Aurelian Church.

Benedictins. Located close to the city center, it welcomes travelers from Paris or other environs.

Also, visually appealing is the Town Hall and its tiered fountain. Built in 1883, the Town Hall houses administrative offices, exhibition and meeting rooms. A gorgeous reception room with a magnificent ceiling in the Town Hall was the site of a reception during our visit.

In the central part of town, the main area for seeing and purchasing Limoges boxes is Boulevard Louis Blanc. Venturing further one can find Haviland's Pavilion de la Porcelaine, located in an industrial zone, south of the Vienne River. The life size "Porcelain Maker" all dressed in china is especially appealing. The Pavilion is open to the public, another treasure found in the city.

Next, one can seek out more of the town's vistas, viewing its centuries' old houses, edifying museums and the Vienne river which cuts through the town and is traversed by a Medieval bridge. Brightly painted or timbered buildings, flowers and decorative ironwork beautify the city. In addition to

*Botanical Gardens*

***Stairs leading to St. Martial's crypt.***

these, Limoges has a variety of little antique shops, restaurants and stores. An open-air antiques market occurs weekly on Rue Brousseau. An interesting stone work archway gently curves overhead as you skirt the Vienne River in Limoges.

For the aficionado, 20 miles to the south is Saint Yrieix La Perche. This is the home of La Seynie (see manufacturer's marks). At this location, there is a museum on porcelain called Musee Les Palloux. In the same complex is a lovely gift shop with some beautiful Limoges boxes.

If you are interested in seeing more porcelain, including boxes, 15 minutes south of Limoges, on the road to Periqueux, is Aixe Sur Vienne. It is home to Maison de la Porcelaine.

*Town Hall and fountains.*

*Art Deco train station—Benedictins.*

*Antique shops, restaurants, and buildings.*

*Architectural features.*

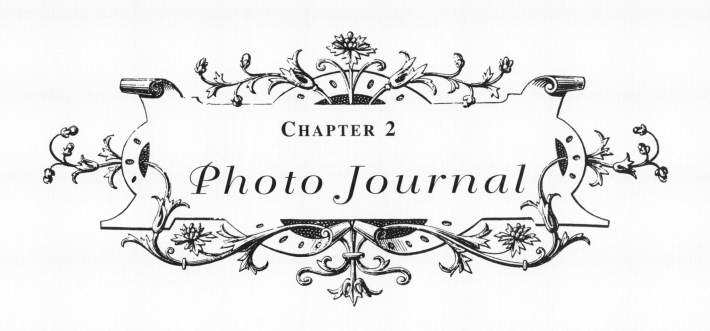

# CHAPTER 2
## Photo Journal

## *Les Classiques*
### (The Classics)

1. Hand-painted square box with a pink trompe l'oeil bow which is alternated with blue sprigged flowers. The clasp is a wreath.

2. A central cartouche enclosing stylized flowers is featured on this hand-painted curved rectangular box. Gilding accents the cartouche and is used in scattered leaf motifs. The curved clasp echoes painted details.

3. A tendrilling bouquet of forget-me-nots is caught up with a pink bow on this hand-painted oval box. The design is continued on the bottom portion of the box. The full-blown flower clasp compliments the design.

4. Purple and blue violas and wisps of wax flower are the focus of this spherical box.

5. *When is an egg not an egg? When it is a fantasy of flowers. Small nosegays are surrounded by a swirling green and gold border. The clasp is a full-faced flower.*

6. *Concentric motifs are featured on this special box. The central motif of johnny-jump-ups is encircled by a gilded leaf design. The outermost motif is the classic oeil-de-perdrix, partridge eye.*

7. *Decorated in the manner of a tapestry, this romantic box is covered with flowers. A golden key accompanies it. Intersecting hearts form the clasp.*

8. *A classically painted lid tops this unusual box. Its base is composed of brass filigree in the form of acanthus leaves, blossoms, and sprays.*

9. Bas-relief roses form the top and clasp of this woven basket. A tiny golden key accompanies it.

10. Three "jeweled" bottles and a funnel are included in this attractively bedecked container. The handles are movable.

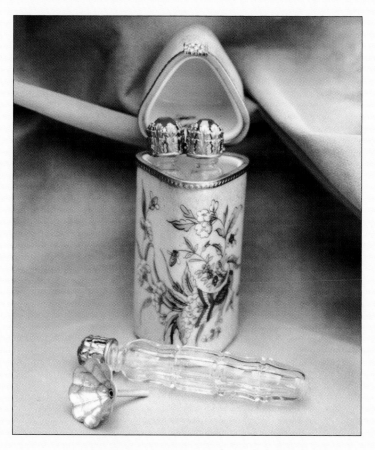

11. A triangular shape and exquisite detail work distinguish this perfume container. Three slender perfume flacons and a funnel complete the set.

12. Blooms cover the top and form the clasp of this lead crystal-based box.

13. **This classic box features a basket overflowing with blooms, a design dating back to the 18th century. The central motif is encircled with exuberant gilded stroke work.**

14. **Flowers of cornflower blue are gathered together on this stunning box. The clasp repeats the motif.**

15. **The vibrant yellow background on this box makes a statement. A medley of flowers are highlighted.**

16. **This perfume bottle is decorated with garlands of flowers bound up with a pink ribbon.**

**18.** This contemporary rendition of a Napoleonic box features the classic motifs: an olive leaf wreath and a bee. The clasp is a simple flower.

**17.** This perfume container is adorned with a gold background accented with gilded highlights; the girth of the bottle is enhanced with a frieze of flowers.

**20.** This unusual fan shape harks back to times when fans were employed with regularity.

**19.** The restrained use of decoration accentuates the raised design on this porcelain box.

21. **This box evokes thoughts of Aphrodite, the Greek goddess of love and beauty, who received a mythical golden apple.**

22. **Pink roses and rose buds adorn this melon fluted hinged box. Gold dots and green swags surround the motifs. The clasp is floral.**

23. **Center stage on this box is a profusion of blooms all tied up with a pink ribbon. The motif is framed by gilding and a swath of royal blue.**

24. **Two miniature handles grace this flower festooned covered vessel. Center stage on this box is a profusion of blooms all tied up with a pink ribbon. Gilding and a swath of royal blue frame the motif.**

**25.** *Rosettes enclosed in gold and green trellising embellish this enchanting oval box.*

**26.** *This dainty oval box is decorated with delicate flowers and a dotted ground in cranberry pink.*

**27.** *A ribbon and a heart-shaped tracery of posies emphasize the shape of this alluring box.*

**28.** *Bodkin containers are traditionally tall and cylindrical, but this antique bodkin fits perfectly in this box. Decorated with ribbons and a fillip of flowers and sealed with a musical clasp this container could hold a variety of sewing implements.*

**29. Six multi-hued butterflies are joined by numerous friendly ladybugs on the surface of this delicately painted spherical container. The accompanying thimble is life-size.**

**30. Slim blue blooms and gold stripes adorn this charming rectangular box. An outstanding feature is the extraordinary pansy clasp.**

**31. A perfume container tucks into this delicately painted egg-shaped box. The soft pink background is punctuated with the classic oeil-de-perdrix motif. The top of the box is decorated with a floral bouquet.**

**32. A multi-dimensional lily of the valley, forget-me-nots and auricula are included in the hand-tied posy on this oval box.**

**33. In order to break up blocks of ground colors visual devises such as cailloute or crazy paving are used. Topping this box is a multicolor floral nosegay.**

**34. In the 18th century some snuff-boxes were made to resemble real items. This modern day version of a book is topped with wire rim spectacles and a quill pen. It is embellished with winsome touches such as ribbons and flowers. A plume serves as the clasp.**

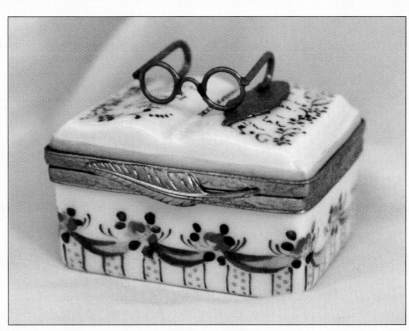

**35. The cupid and dove on this intricately hand-painted box, evoke a feeling of love. A brass heart seals it.**

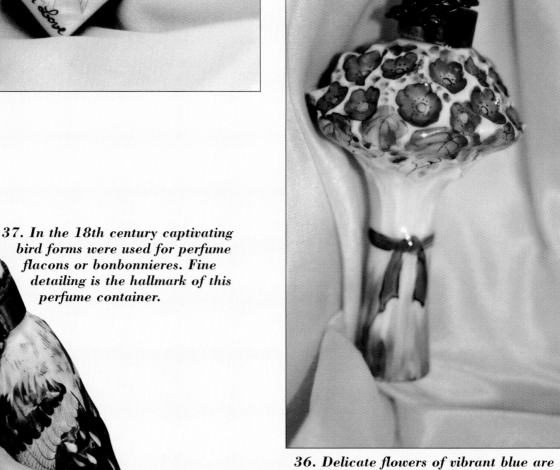

**37. In the 18th century captivating bird forms were used for perfume flacons or bonbonnieres. Fine detailing is the hallmark of this perfume container.**

**36. Delicate flowers of vibrant blue are tied up in this bouquet. This piece is done in the style of an antique porcelain perfume flacon. The collar, chain and crown fretwork is brass.**

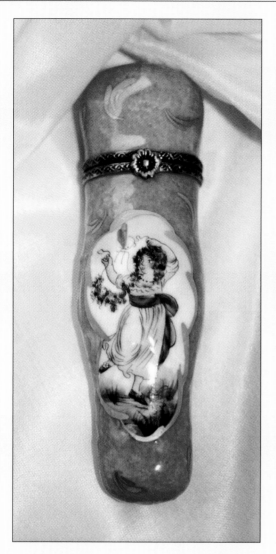

39. *Pink and blue flowers embrace this tender expression of affection.*

38. *The woman portrayed on this beautiful etui is almost palpable.*

40. *This miniature envelope is adorned with flowers and tender thoughts. Upon opening this gesture of love one finds a missive which reads "...Sealed with a Kiss."*

41. *In times gone by motto boxes like this were given to friends and lovers.*

# Pour Une Occasion Speciale
## (Special Occasions)

**42. Chilled champagne is provided for the fin de siecle, a once-in-a-lifetime experience. Inscribed in this box is the notation, "2000—A year to remember." Exquisite detailing distinguishes this exceptional box.**

**43. This box held Marian's engagement ring when Glenn proposed. A garland of roses and forget-me-nots encircles their names.**

**44. Two figures meet in a kiss in this ode to budding romance on this lovely hand-painted box.**

**45. Ribbons and blooms surround this sweet expression of love.**

46. *Sweet thoughts of love are bespoken. Pink roses and blue daisies embrace the heart-felt sentiment. Gold stroke work serves as an accent.*

47. *A loving bride and groom under an arch form the top of this three-tiered wedding cake. Flowers encircle and cascade from this impressive box. Two hearts united, fittingly, are the clasp.*

48. *Just Married. Here is a stretch limousine supplied with all the accouterments for celebration.*

49. Whether it's for baby's first birthday or a subsequent time, birthday cheer is here for the enjoying.

50. What an angelic idea. This precious cherub comes to express Valentine's wishes to be remembered throughout the years.

51. The luck of the Irish may be held within this creation. This heart-shaped box features a four-leaf clover surrounded by purple and orange flowers.

52. Beautifully molded and finely detailed, this adorable duo of rabbits seem to be discussing where to hide the Easter eggs.

**53. Any mother would appreciate the sentiment enclosed in this flower-bedecked envelope.**

**54. Pride of accomplishment is conveyed by this box. It is topped with a mortarboard and tassel. Fittingly, a diploma is included. Hands shake in congratulations on this brass clasp.**

**55. July 4th is a time of pride. We celebrate it by flying the red, white, and blue.**

**56. This delightful Halloween box features a witch intent on mixing up a magic brew.**

**57. Thanksgiving is exemplified by the horn of plenty, the cornucopia.  Nature's bounty seemingly pours forth from this box.**

**58. Thoughts of warm family gatherings are brought to mind when looking at this Thanksgiving turkey box.**

**59. History and tradition are represented in this beautifully painted figural box.**

**60. The menorah is a symbol of Chanukah, the festival of lights.**

**61. The Star of David serves as the clasp of this beautiful Dreidel.**

**62. Sprigs of Holly decorate the base of this snowcapped Christmas tree. A gold star tops it off.**

**63. Symbols of Christmas abound on this festive cup and saucer. A brass spoon serves as the clasp.**

**64. Tassels and holly are richly painted in red and green on this holiday box.**

**65. Multi-leveled and brightly decorated, this holiday box features Santa riding a train and waving hello.**

**66. Christmas songs come to mind when looking at this drum-shaped box. A French horn decorated with holly and ribbons adorns the top.**

# *Bon Appetit*
## (Epicurean Delights)

**67. This piece offers three strawberries so luscious you can almost taste them. The clasp is a bee.**

**68. This sumptuous Charlotte russe is dotted with cherries. The clasp is made up of two ripe cherries.**

**69. Ripe, ample peaches overflow from this woven basket. Brass handles complete the theme.**

**70. This basket contains a melange of fruit; the profusion includes a pineapple, pears, apricots, grapes and other delights. Its intricate clasp is a basket overflowing with flowers.**

71. The chef's toque is topped with cascading fruits.

72. A tempting tart filled with a cluster of plump, choice strawberries. A brass bee has come to visit.

73. Striations of pink garnish this radish. A brass bunny serves as the clasp.

74. A clasp in the guise of a bee has lighted upon this woven basket. It is loaded with asparagus, eggplant, cabbage and other vegetables which could make a lovely bouquet of hors d'oeuvres.

75. Whether called an aubergine or eggplant this beautiful purple vegetable is very appealing.

76. You can almost taste the mellow flavor of this ripe avocado.

78. The pomegranate and its jewel seeds form the basis of many cultures' lore.

77. This petite plate of asparagus offers us the texture, color and almost the taste of this appealing vegetable.

**80. Strawberries, pears and grapes embellish the top of this picnic basket. Its movable brass handle makes it easier to carry.**

**79. Fresh fruits and vegetables are sheltered by a brightly striped awning on this charming "rolling" fruit cart. The canopy supports, handles, hinge and floral basket clasp are brass.**

**81. Lifelike in form and texture, this young artichoke is studded with tightly packed leaves. This culinary temptation is richly painted in greens and purples.**

**82. Upon opening, this pea pod reveals numerous plump green peas.**

**83. Bursting with white florets, this cauliflower appears as if it is fresh from the field.**

**84. When you lift the dome on this beautifully hand-painted box, you find a cheese board topped with three-dimensional cheeses.**

**85. Topped with Gouda and Swiss cheese, this box provides treats for the international palate. A brass knife is at the ready.**

**86. An assortment of cheeses tempts your appetite.**

**87.** *Nature's bounty in a bottle. In this wonderful hand-painted basket you have your choice of red or white wine.*

**88.** *This box could be a reminder of a romantic evening with a loved one spent eating pasta and drinking wine.*

**89.** *This handsome wine serving basket complete with a bottle of Bordeaux is accented with a brass handle, and a grape cluster clasp.*

**90.** *Green and red grapes with tendrilling vines and multicolored leaves grace the top of this beautifully detailed and textured basket. Fittingly, grapes form the clasp.*

**91. Covered with a sumptuous array of vegetables, this tureen is a reminder of stews made in 18th century France (Pot d'oille).**

**92. These glistening green grapes are symbolic of a harvest's bounty. When this cluster of grapes is turned over one discovers the box is a full bunch of grapes.**

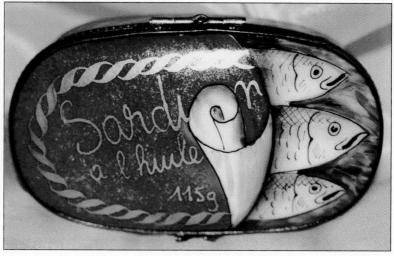

**94. This box offers "Beluga caviar" you can savor at any time.**

**93. When one uncurls the top of this brightly-colored "tin," three delicious sardines are revealed.**

95. *An impressive addition to any buffet table, this salmon platter is garnished with large shrimp, avocado and egg.*

96. *Layers of almond paste and apricot jam alternate with pastry in this miniature Napoleon. A brass spoon lays in wait on a porcelain plate bordered with gold and blue.*

97. *This box is shaped like an old fashion tea caddy and harkens us back to a time when tea was an expensive commodity, shipped from far away exotic lands.*

98. *This chef's hat whisks us right into the kitchen.*

**99.** *Rust-colored Iceland poppies float on the surface of this wonderful veilleuse. Its name is derived from the French term for night vigil.*

**100.** *This hand-painted box offers a luscious dessert of fresh pears presented on a plate decorated with dainty blue flowers.*

**101.** *Tea is served! This gorgeous tea set is presented on a galleried tray. The decorative edging, handles, hinge and spoon clasp are brass.*

**102.** *Slicing open this sweet orange fleshed melon is the beginning of a tasteful experience.*

**103. We can almost taste the sweetness of this apple slice.**

**104. A delicious sliced apple sits atop this delicately decorated plate.**

**105. This comport holds compote made with an array of different fruits. The clasp is a luxurious bunch of grapes.**

**106. Fresh fruits cascade over the top of this dual hinged picnic basket. Delicately tinted fruit is shown against both white and gilded backgrounds.**

**107.** *This miniature porcelain footed bowl is laden with enticing fruits.*

**108.** *Strawberry jam, croissants, a soft-boiled egg and tea are inviting arranged on this pink trimmed tray.*

**109.** *This tiny stack of profiteroles appears to be topped with chocolate sauce and dabs of cream. The pink and gold plate comes with a spoon. The bow clasp peeks out from below the plate.*

**110.** *With a background color as soft as dandelion tufts, this tureen also features a classic floral motif, the oeil-de-perdrix motif and accent gilding. A simple brass bow clasp ties it together.*

# Le Jardin
## (The Garden)

**111. Snowball-shaped hydrangeas of various hues grace a delightful terra cotta pot. The clasp is a rose.**

**112. This lovely white hyacinth box actually holds a perfume vial.**

**113. This adorable tableau shows a bunny stopped at an arbored garden gate.**

**114. An angelic visitor is ensconced in a bed of delicately painted pansies.**

**115.** *A classic Lutyens bench, topped with a hat and bouquet, is sheltering a bed of tulips. Will the people return for their belongings?*

**116.** *A blooming strawberry plant and its fruit are featured on this curvaceous watering can. The clasp is a leaf.*

**117.** *The cover of this miniature gardening book features an ironwork arbor covered with an abundance of flowers. In addition, a large terra cotta pot is shown overflowing with a profusion of blooms. Included in this box are diminutive gardening tools.*

**118. Green trellising and a basket of fruit adorn this appealing watering can. The clasp is a trophy of gardening tools.**

**119. This bouquet of orange anemones is seemingly held together by its matching ribbon.**

**120. A network of gold veining highlights this rich green leaf. A bright red ladybug has come to visit.**

**122. This morning glory glimmers as if it were sprinkled by dew.**

**121. Blue and yellow are a charming contrast on this appealing pansy.**

**123.** *The face of this gently blooming rose is painted in shades of yellow.*

**125.** *One can almost see this ethereal orange poppy waft in the breeze.*

**124.** *This stunning blue flower features a bee looking for pollen.*

**126.** *An ode to springtime; this heart shaped box is covered with flowers, and mama and papa birds celebrating their prospective offspring. The clasp is entwined hearts.*

**127.** *Gradations of yellow enhance this wonderful rose bud.*

128. Perky multi-colored flowers line up on this hand-painted watering can.
The brass snail is gliding past the procession.

129. Splashy colors paint the face of this miniature Stargazer lily.

131. Gardening on a spring day is brought to mind by this lovely pot and garden tools. It is delightfully decorated with a hand-painted ribboned hat blowing in the breeze amid a shower of roses.

130. This wheelbarrow holds the makings of a wonderful salad. A trophy of gardening tools serves as the clasp.

132. *Lilies of the valley bob their heads on this appealing box. When opened it reveals a porcelain heart pendant with a matching theme. Hearts entwined form the clasp.*

133. *Two hand-painted birds inhabit this floral arbor. The clasp is a trophy of gardening tools.*

134. *On this box we see honey bees, in painted and brass form returning to the skep, a twisted straw hive.*

135. *Squirrelly for nuts? This miniature walnut has lots of texture. The clasp is a bloom.*

136. *A ladybug tarrys on this curvaceous acorn and its oak leaf.*

# Les Animaux
## (The Animals)

**138. An adorable kitten has a little mealtime mishap. The clasp is a flowing ribbon.**

**137. This championship Boxer comes prepared. When opened a hand-painted boxing ring is revealed. The clasp is a crown.**

**139. This butterfly just fluttered by to visit this inquisitive Bichon Frise.**

**140. The beautifully detailed West Highland Terrier box is decorated with a bone and a grassy field. The clasp is a bow.**

**141. This comely Maltese has all the items necessary for primping.**

**142. Mom and her kitten snuggle contentedly in this picture of feline felicity. The clasp is a broad-winged butterfly.**

**143. Blue ribbons bedeck this appealing Dachshund and his barrel-shaped stand.**

**144. What will the outcome be, pal or palate? The fish clasp echoes the theme.**

**145. Nestled underneath this mama hen are two adorable yellow chicks.**

**146. One can almost feel the wind blowing when looking at this galloping horse.**

**147. Sitting on top of the world, this contented chicken is comfortably settled on a stone and squashed mortar fence. Moss and greenery add to the detailing.**

**148. With her long blond hair safely braided out of the way, this maid can attend to her task. The Holstein cow seems pleased. The clasp echoes the theme.**

**149. This darling tabby appears to be guarding a precious item.**

**150. This billy goat has fresh hay for lunch.**

**151. A delightful frog is seemingly about to emit a sonorous croak.**

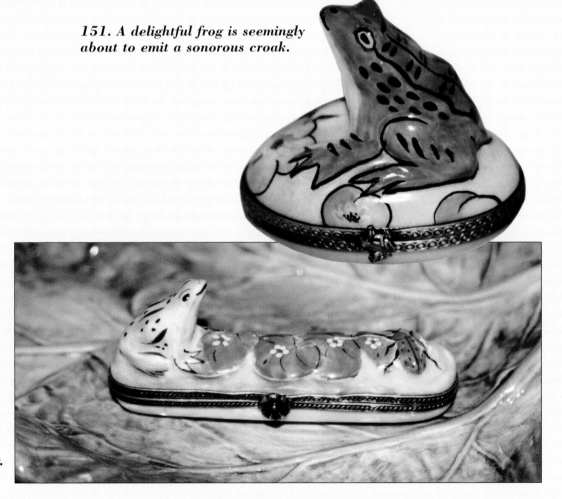

**152. This lovely oval box sports a lily pond setting inhabited by a frisky frog and an inquisitive beetle. The clasp is a flower.**

**154. Majestic colors grace this beautifully molded pheasant.**

**153. Gliding on its glistening track this snail greets the day.**

**156. This duo of ducks is swimming through cattails. The clasp is a duck.**

**155. Poking its head from beneath its protective green plates, this turtle basks in the sun.**

157. *With its head seemingly bent in question, this deftly painted owl is perched on a piece of wood, with the moon and stars reflected in the water below.*

158. *A momma penguin and her chick on an ice floe, a chilling experience.*

159. *A sweet dessert shared by two. These blue birds are snacking on a luscious cherry.*

160. *The mother swan's white plumage is contrasted by her cygnet's fluffy down. The inside of this box is decorated with a nest occupied by two eggs.*

161. This stately eagle is perched atop a fallen branch.

163. Tucked safely in his mother's pouch this joey can go on any journey.

162. Mountainous terrains come to mind upon looking at this proud ram.

164. This adorable, furry koala cub clutches his mom.

165. Painted a beautiful tawny yellow, this tiger rests majestically.

166. Peacefully awaiting the long trek ahead, this camel is painted in the eponymous color.

167. Waiting on the grassy shore, this alligator is ready to glide into the water.

168. This box is painted in colors as soft as a morning mist. Woodland berries grow in the vicinity of this cozy fox.

**169.** *In wide-eyed wonderment this perky bunny enjoys a delectable lunch.*

**170.** *Alert to his surroundings, this fox looks as if he could bolt at a moment's notice.*

**171.** *The top of this bonbonniere showcases an auburn-colored squirrel industriously gathering nuts.*

**172.** *Dressed in denim overalls this adorable beaver is ready for work.*

**173. This intricately detailed monkey is dressed in elegant gold and red attire. His clasp is a peach.**

**174. A tropical fish swimming in a glass bowl is the focus of this unusual fantasy box.**

**175. This sleek dolphin is leaping gracefully through the cresting waves.**

**176. Colorations evocative of a tropical reef embellish this fish. One can imagine it darting through the corals.**

## Pour Les Petits
### (For The Little Ones)

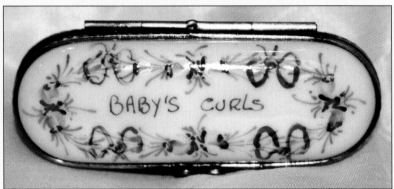

**177.** *Precious memories can be safely tucked away in this flower and ribbon trimmed box.*

**178.** *Shh, baby is asleep. A sweet baby is napping contentedly in this canopied bassinet.*

**179.** *This oval box provides a secure home for an enduring reminder from baby's first haircut; crosshatching and flowers form the decoration.*

**180.** *What a lovely way to revisit this Old Mother Goose rhyme. This charming fiddle playing cat is one of the details on this box.*

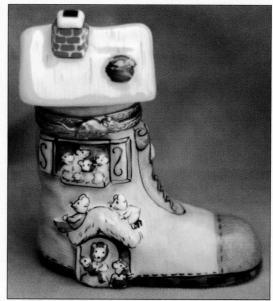

**182. This rendition of the old woman in a shoe is packed with interest.**

**181. A spacious orange pumpkin, resting atop an open book of nursery rhymes, serves as the abode of Peter Pumpkineater's wife.**

**184. This sweet teddy is all dressed up, he even has epaulets on his jacket. When the box is opened a tiny bear is revealed.**

**183. The pleasures of childhood return while looking at this box. The two well-dressed teddy bears are playing on this movable teeter-totter.**

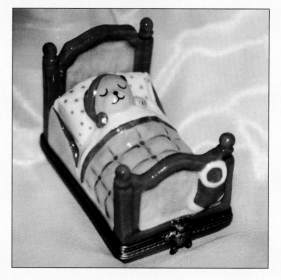

**185. An adorable sleepy time bear.**

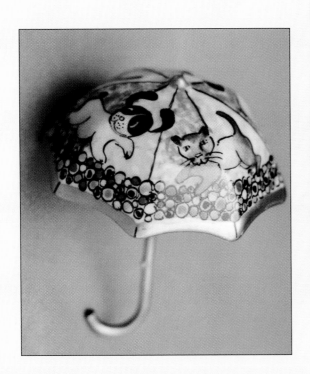

**187. Noah's Ark is filled to capacity with its pairs of animals. The central cabin is removable.**

*186. It's raining cats and dogs.*

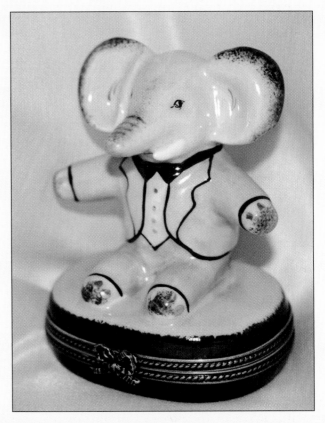

**188. A heart-shaped nose and delicately detailed eyes grace the face of this bunny. He is all dressed up for a night on the town and is bringing a fat carrot to share with his date.**

*189. Tusk, tusk. This elegant elephant is ready for any occasion.*

**190. This thought provoking box reminds one of Dr. Seuss' fable about Yertle the Turtle.**

**191. Three little kittens cavort and search for their mittens on this wonderful box.**

**192. The theme of speak no evil, hear no evil, see no evil is whimsically carried out on this unusual box.**

**193. This diminutive Dalmatian appears to be concentrating on setting up a shot.**

194. *I scream, you scream, we all scream for ice cream. With hot summer weather, the ice cream truck provides a wonderful relief.*

195. *Can this gymnast bear the competition? Performing on the pommel horse is difficult.*

196. *A, B, C blocks are scattered around the base of this charming red engine.*

197. *This brightly hand-painted open toy box is overflowing with delights. The box has a teddy bear closure.*

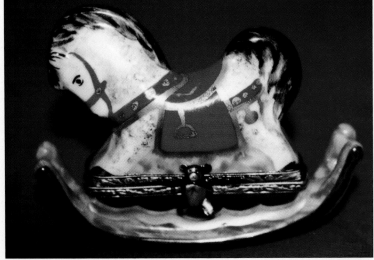

198. *Childhood memories come to mind when you view this hand-painted rocking horse box. A teddy bear clasp finishes the piece.*

# *En Voyage*
## (Traveling)

**200.** *One can see the steel framework of this Paris landmark detailed in this beautifully hand-painted miniature. The clasp is the Arc de Triomphe.*

**199.** *Six molded and painted lions majestically serve as the support for this impressive globe. The blue of the oceans contrasts beautifully against the colorful landmasses. A regal lion clasp roams the equator.*

**201.** *We can see that this hatbox is well traveled. It has the stickers to prove it.*

**202. With its majestic presence, Paris' Arc de Triomphe (the world's largest triumphal arch) makes a bold statement.**

**203. Beautifully molded and intricately detailed, this replica of the Notre Dame Cathedral has little brass bells in its belfries.**

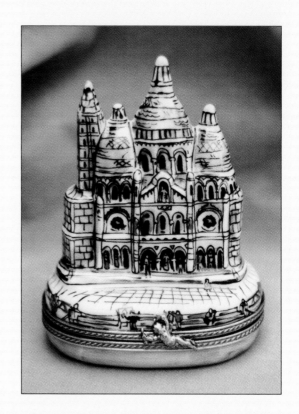

**204. This pyramid atrium provides entrance to the Louvre.**

**205. Sacre Coeur is the subject of this wonderfully detailed box. The clasp is an angel in flight.**

**206.** *Located in the Loire Valley, the Chateau de Chenonceau features arches, turrets and a tower. The chateau is built partially over the Cher River. A wandering minstrel is the clasp.*

**207.** *A delightful train emerges from a tunnel on this multi-dimensional box. The clasp is a stylized bow.*

**209.** *This Queen chess piece is magnificently hand-painted. The clasp is a fleur-de-lys.*

**208.** *This regal fleur-de-lys is a present day representation of the symbol of three lilies tied together.*

**210.** *Jewel colors are the hallmark of this stately crown.*

**211.** *A kingly mien is projected in this piece.*

**212.** *One of the enduring symbols of London, Big Ben, is captured timelessly in porcelain.*

**213.** *This unique box features a castle which encloses a courtyard and fountain. A number of hinges allow for different views. A knight in armor serves as a clasp*

**214.** *This handsomely painted windmill box includes shuttered windows and a curved doorway. It also features "red sail cloth" blades.*

**215.** *At the doorway of a rural home in the Netherlands, one might find klompen, wooden shoes.*

**216.** *The Egyptian pyramids are a wondrous achievement. This miniature replica with its golden highlights speaks to the splendor of the pharaohs.*

**217. The Egyptian Sphinx is a testament to the Pharaoh's prowess. This subtly molded box is boldly painted in blue and gold.**

**218. Lovely detail work adorns this tome on ancient Egypt.**

**219. The Sydney Opera House is such a distinctive landmark.**

**220.** *Days enjoyed, adventures experienced and noted to be savored at a more leisurely time.*

**221.** *On this box, a beautifully painted coconut tree shades a little grass shack. Enclosed in the box is a porcelain fish.*

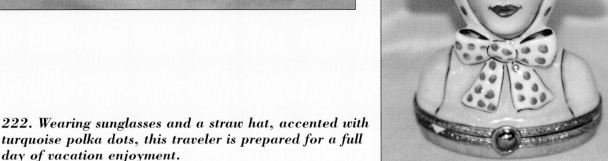

**222.** *Wearing sunglasses and a straw hat, accented with turquoise polka dots, this traveler is prepared for a full day of vacation enjoyment.*

223. This exuberantly hand-painted box is decorated with dash, and sports a bottle of suntan lotion. The clasp is a large tropical flower which echoes the bag's motif.

224. This hand-painted bathing beauty is never going to get a sunburn. Lovely detail work offers her sandals, sunglasses and lotion. The clasp is a boat.

225. Washington D.C.'s most famous landmark, The White House. This box captures the distinctive character of this historic building.

**226. This box takes us to New York City to visit the Empire State Building. One can imagine the bustling traffic on 5th Avenue.**

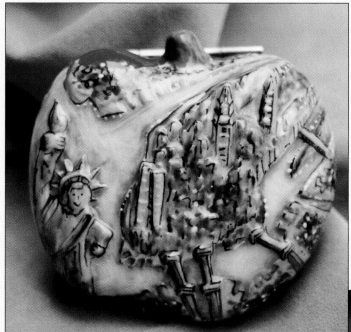

**227. Whether you call it New York or The Big Apple this city pulsates with activity. A miniature yellow cab is inside.**

**228.** *The lighthouse looms over nearby buildings. Its inhabitants are ever vigilant in saving ships from danger. A unique feature of this box is its double clasps. A striped life preserver can be found inside.*

**229.** *San Francisco's Golden Gate Bridge impressively crosses this box. Inside is another famous mode of transportation associated with the city.*

230. *Pebble Beach, California, is the scene of this wonderful golf course. There is even a golf cart available for use. The clasp is a golf bag and clubs.*

231. *The owner of this backpack seems to be in touch with the yin and yang of life.*

232. *Ever want to see a western filmed? Here is a Hollywood production in progress. The clasp is a baseball cap (like those worn on location).*

233. *This set of hand-painted boxes is straight out of Hollywood.*
*(A) Chair  (B) Camera*

# *Moyens de Transport*
## (Transportation)

*234. Italian opera being sung by a Venetian gondolier comes to mind.*

*235. This steamship is cresting the waves on its venture. The ship is beautifully hand-painted with the striking contrast of black and red. Fittingly, the clasp is a helm.*

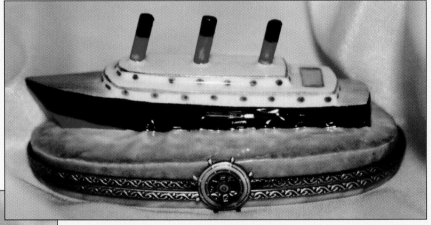

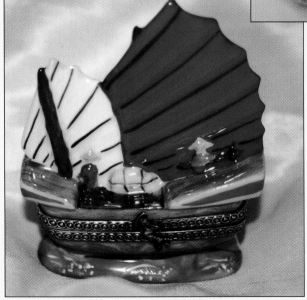

*236. This colorful Chinese junk sails swiftly down the river.*

**237. Blue billowing waves are beneath this brightly-colored sailboat.**

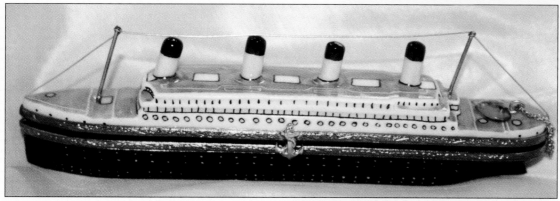

**238. Here is a box of Titanic importance.**

**239. One can view London from this delightful red double bus without fear of getting wet.**

240. This distinctive taxi is ubiquitous in London. Roomy and painted a decorous black it appears ready to pick up passengers.

241. This 1930 Packard Roadster harks back to times gone by.

242. "The mail must go through." This pony express driver is upholding that age-old motto.

**243.** *This yellow school bus stops at all memories.*

**244.** *One can imagine this engine, which is equipped with a cowcatcher, traveling across scenic routes in times gone by. The clasp is a stylized bow motif.*

**245.** *This bright red gas pump takes us back to a time before automation and high gas prices.*

**246.** *Mentally when you hop on this motorcycle, you can experience the wind in your face and the exhilaration of the ride.*

247. This box is an exciting red dune buggy.

248. Take off into the wild blue yonder in this single propeller plane.

249. Detailed modeling and painting are the hallmark of this airport box.

**250.** *Ready to take off at a moment's notice. This helicopter sports a brass propeller and landing mechanism.*

**251.** *Seemingly counting down to blast off, this rocket is in the ready position on the launch pad.*

**252.** *The Space Shuttle, Orbiter, is posed on the top of a globe in this testament to space exploration.*

**253.** *The excitement of the space race is brought to mind by this detailed replica of the Apollo module.*

# *Beaux Arts*
## (Fine Arts)

*254. Group of six—these boxes pay homage to the works of Matisse, Monet and Lautrec.*

**255. HRH Prince Charles set up an organization entitled the Prince's Trust, to help disadvantaged young people. In 1995 the UK Mask Campaign began, setting into motion a project which generated hundreds of Masks created by celebrities and artists. Thirty of those masks were done in limited edition in Limoges porcelain. Shown here are the Anthony Hopkins and Barry Manilow boxes.**

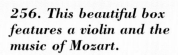

**256. This beautiful box features a violin and the music of Mozart.**

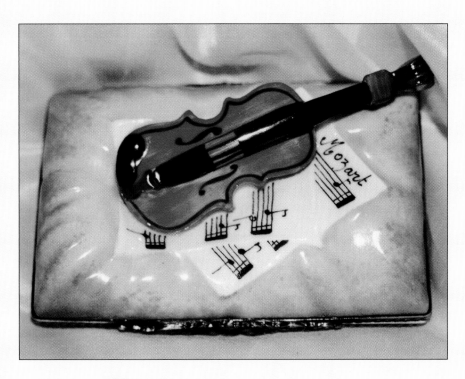

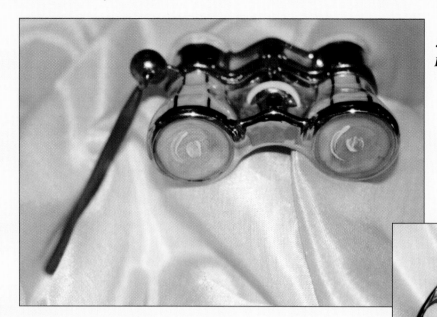

**257. This lorgnette is exquisitely painted.**

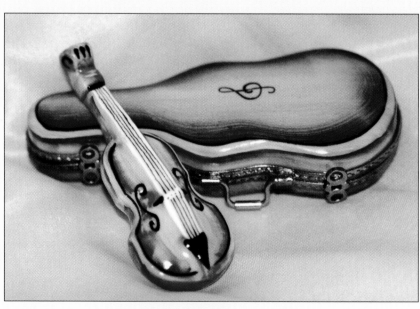

**258. A musical trophy serves as the centerpiece of this button-shaped box, raised gold C-scrolls highlight the design.**

**259. An angelic sound is emitted by the harp.**

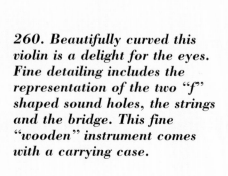

**260. Beautifully curved this violin is a delight for the eyes. Fine detailing includes the representation of the two "f" shaped sound holes, the strings and the bridge. This fine "wooden" instrument comes with a carrying case.**

**261.** *This grand piano is festooned with an abundance of ribbons and flowers.*

**262.** *Listen for the dulcet tones of the French horn.*

**263.** *These miniature tomes are highlighted with faux-tooled bindings.*

**264. This upright piano is entrancingly decorated to continue the music theme. The clasp is a lyre with sheet music interwoven.**

**265. Comfortably curved, this artist's palette has paints ready for mixing.**

**266. Priming for a day of painting begins with this blue paint tube.**

267. Beginning in the 16th century troupes of actors performed impromptu plays. A stock player in the commedia dell' arte was Harlequin.

268. A musical theme is the keynote of this box; tones of russet, pink and blue tumble forth.

269. Sitting at an easel one can contemplate and paint many things. An artist's brush and palette are painted inside. A brass fleur-de-lys is the clasp.

270. Three perfume bottles are enclosed in this delicate blue trunk, enhanced by a classical musical trophy.

*271. Animal orchestras in porcelain date back to the 18th century. This bass fiddle playing frog appears quite comfortable in his tux jacket and polka dot pants.*

*272. This fiddling frog could travel to any event and entertain. His natty attire and apparent poise set him apart.*

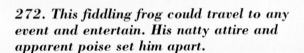

*273. This cello-playing frog is a symphony of satorial splendor.*

92

# *Sport de Plein Air*
## (Sports)

**274.** *This lion tennis player is not about to miss that ball.*

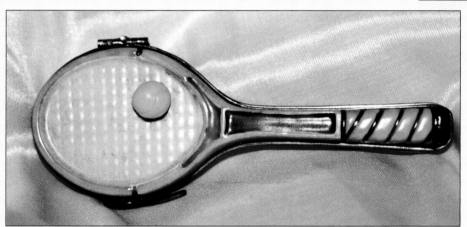

**275.** *Don't you just love it? You are always ready to serve with this delightful box.*

**276.** *This speedy fellow is in the blocks and prepared for the race.*

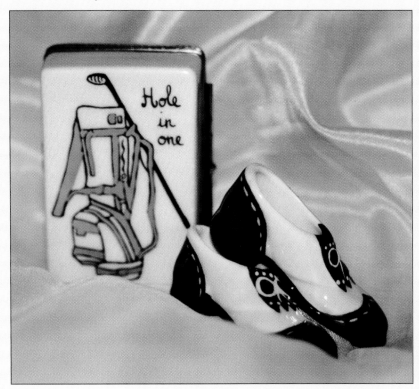

*277. A pair of comfortable golf shoes is included in this delightful golf-related box.*

*279. This golf bag is filled with clubs and is at the ready for a day of golf.*

*278. This driver and ball serve as a reminder of enjoyable days spent golfing.*

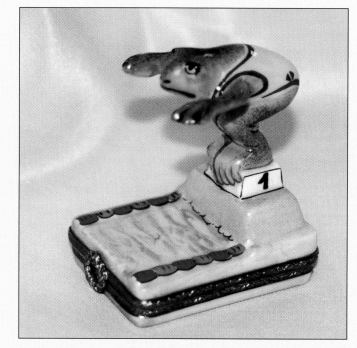

**280.** *Let the race begin. This frog is ready to dive right in.*

**281.** *Croquet anyone? This unusual box has three striped mallets ready for a smashing game.*

**282.** *This woven box's interior contains the necessary fishing gear. The clasp is a fish.*

**283. This lighthearted hand-painted creel shows pictorially the fish that got away.**

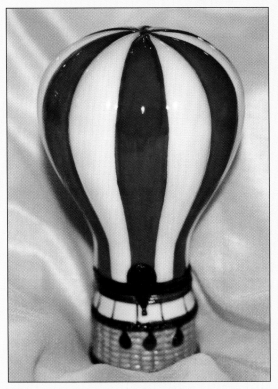

**284. This box is a reminder of the French ballooning efforts that occurred at the end of the 1700s.**

**285. Mountaineering requires courage, perseverance and stamina.**

**286. Wonderful times spent skating are brought to mind by this sleek skate.**

## *La Mode* (Fashion)

**287. This box takes the form of a portrait neckline enhanced with jewels and a soft pink rose.**

**288. This handbag is delicately painted with ribbons and garlands of roses. It is finished with a fine-gauge chain strap and a bow clasp.**

**289. A pink ribbon and flowers top this charming hat. Blue scallops and stroke work finish the hand-painted detailing.**

**290.** *This vibrant, polka-dotted chapeau will never lack attention.*

**291.** *Faux pearls and a ribbon bow are added to the hand-painted touches on this distinctive neckline box.*

**292.** *This charming bag features blue and gold latticework surrounding a multitude of flowers.*

**293.** *Whether for storage or show, this box makes organizing your shoes easier. Intricate detailing is evidenced on the shoes and case. A stylized bow closure finishes it off.*

**294.** *A leopard skin patterned corset is featured on this dressmaker's mannequin. Brass accents include a footed stand, the hinge and the scissors clasp.*

**295.** *There is nothing pedestrian about this shoebox, which is equipped with a movable display rack. Matching shoes are included.*

**296. Featuring flowers and foliage this fetching summer hat provides more than protection. The brass clasp is a detailed flower.**

**297. Haute couture. Paris frocks are fitted on mannequins like this.**

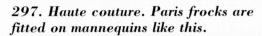

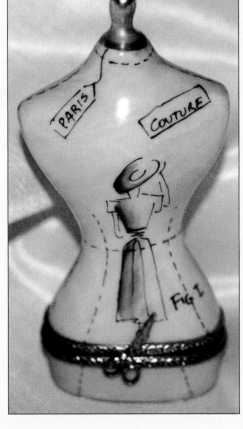

**298. Whether you call it a purse or a handbag, this hand-painted box has lots of verve. This creation is painted in gold, deep purple, sunshine yellow and a variety of pinks. The clasp is a bow.**

**299.** *One can imagine dancing the night away in this flower festooned dress.*

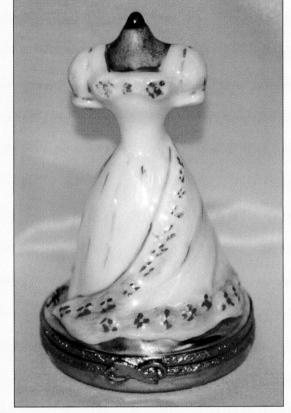

**300.** *A shower of roses embellishes this hat. Tying it together is a brass bow clasp.*

**301.** *This fantasy box is in the form of an ornately embroidered shoe with a "jeweled" bucket. The hinge and clasp are on the heel.*

# Messages
## (Communication)

*302. Across or Down? This clever boite features a crossword puzzle.*

*Inside of piece.*

*303. I LOVE YOU. A message you can never hear too much.*

**304.** *A delicately flowered telephone is ensconced on the top of this skirted table. The skirt's drape is punctuated with tiers of fabric and tassels.*

**306. Want to make a call in London? This telephone box is the place to go.**

**305. Shiny black and sturdy this phone dates from the time before push button and cellular phones. A pen-shaped clasp is a fitting connection.**

**307. Communication starts with the word, sometimes typewritten or typeset, it opens us up to the world.**

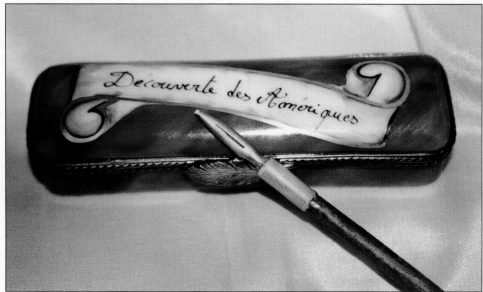

**308. This scroll proclaims the Discovery of the Americas, a "nibbed pen" is enclosed.**

**309. The Declaration of Independence is just as moving today as when it was written on July 4, 1776. This miniature document features a scroll shape, wire rim glasses and a handsome quill pen.**

**310. This evocative tableau contains a trompe l' oeil malachite stamp box which is both beautiful and useful. The clasp is a royal looking lion.**

**311. With this pen one can sign a contract, write a book or compose any number of things.**

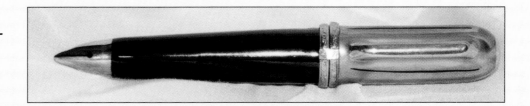

**312. This inkwell is beautifully decorated in the classic manner.**

# *Mobilier Miniature*
## (Furnishings)

*314. This fantastic serving cart is supplied with delicately painted porcelain cups and saucers. Hand painting is evidenced on every surface, beginning with the top, and its decorative place mats and inviting croissants. The second shelf contains more croissants, a rose and a pair of spectacles for reading the accompanying book and missives. Upon opening the box, one finds hand-painted fruit. The cart's handles, hinges, rolling wheels and bow clasp are brass.*

*313. This attractive side table supports a lustrous silver bowl, which is overflowing with a variety of tempting fruits.*

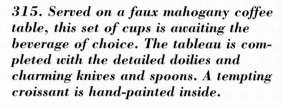

*315. Served on a faux mahogany coffee table, this set of cups is awaiting the beverage of choice. The tableau is completed with the detailed doilies and charming knives and spoons. A tempting croissant is hand-painted inside.*

**316.** *This delightful box has many features. The skirted table is set for guests and topped with a gold bowl overflowing with roses. Braided brass posts support the brightly striped canopy, edged with large rosettes and tassels. Finally, it is surrounded by a garden of flowers. The clasp is fittingly a rose.*

**317.** *Tea for two. This box presents an intimate setting for whatever will transpire.*

**318.** *A view with a room. This unusual box allows us another perspective.*

107

319. With all the necessary equipment available, this writing desk beckons. "Golden spectacles" can be found inside.

320. Pitcher, basin, and soap dish are stationed atop this marble covered washstand. A towel and mitt come inside.

321. This vanity table's equipage includes a wig stand, wig, powder box and perfume atomizer. A folded pink towel comes inside.

*322. A burgundy toile de Jouy print is featured on this comfortable chair. For complete contentment a burgundy pillow has been added. The clasp is a bow.*

*323. This box is a miniature Sabbath table.*

*324. This ornate washstand has everything ready for morning ablutions. Pink roses decorate the porcelain accessory pieces, one of which is a tiny vanity box.*

**325. What a lovely armoire! It is packed with colorful items and even has a faux mirror.**

**326. This delightful skirted table is set for guests and supplied with a chilled bucket of champagne and a setting for an intimate dinner. Intertwined hearts form the clasp.**

**327. Based on an 18th century theme, this box shows a couple in bed. He wears a striped nightcap but she leaves her blond hair loose. The bedding features a floral comforter and coordinating bed skirt.**

## *Merveilles Cachees*
### (Hidden Treasures)

328. The bowed front adds a sensual feel to this box, which is awash with wonderful details. Masses of flowers decorate its top, front, sides and back. The cobalt blue gives an intense backdrop to the central floral design. Banding the box is a medley of flowers. When the box is opened it reveals a gold interior holding three blue "jeweled" bottles. The clasp is an ornate wreath motif.

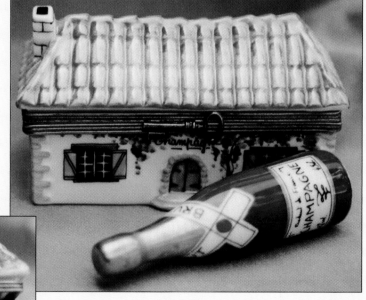

329. Champagne house! Locked away to be opened with a brass key, this box contains a bottle of champagne.

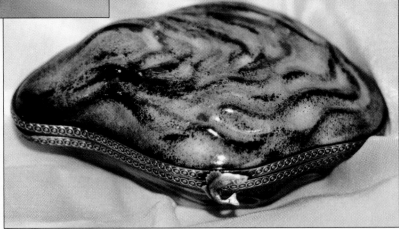

*Top of box.*

**330. A special wooden crate is the home of two removable bottles of French wine.**

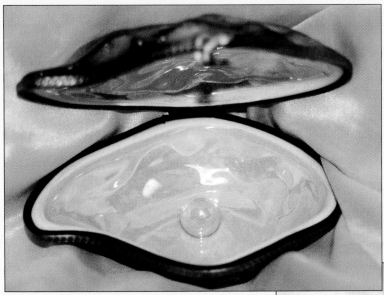

**331. This oyster shaped box is hand-painted with waves of variations in both color and texture on its shell. When opened you find a pearl on its luminescent ground.**

**332.** Your garden party will be fully accessorized when this delightful box's contents are used. This box ingeniously has a brass spoon as a support mechanism. The handles, hinge and stylized bow clasp are also brass.

**333.** This exquisitely executed footed box takes the form of a gilded cage enclosing two beautifully plumed birds. When the box is opened a lovely molded bird is revealed. Perhaps the mother bird is attempting to feed the baby. The clasp is a double heart.

334. A hummingbird in flight is arrestingly hand painted on this wonderful inkwell. In the front portion of the top of this semi-circular box is an indentation for a pen. When you open the cap to the inkwell you find a thimble-like reservoir. Topping and surrounding the ink cap are hand-painted ribbons and flowers. The clasp is a butterfly in flight.

335. Regal colors and motifs cover this egg shaped box. When it is opened it reveals a scallop enclosing a pearl.

**336. Noah has a lot of company on this Ark. Details abound and animals run riot both inside and out, on this unusual box. Three-dimensional animals use the portholes for viewing. Both sides of the box have hinged portions which swing open to reveal four more areas populated with other inhabitants. Seahorses serve as clasps.**

**337. Molded to look like a tree house, this hinged box opens to reveal a homey scene.**

## Collections Precieuses
### (Assemblages)

The items depicted in this section are not included in the price list at the chapter's end. This section is designed to show you some different ways to display your most treasured boxes. A few favorite ways are to group them by shape, color, and theme. Arranging your boxes is a delightful way to enjoy your collection.

*Please join us for tea.*

*This is a close-up of an antique cake carrier holding Limoges boxes.*

*Time stands still when you appreciate this evocative tableau.*

*Callioute, also called crazy paving, is the predominant motif used on this purple box shown in the garden.*

117

*This window seat serves up a sampling of Limoges goodies.*

*Purple and yellow connects this group.*

*This shot from an antique dealer's home has a turn-of-the-century Limoges powder box.*

*This bathroom setting incorporates Limoges boxes.*

*An appealing array.*

*One woman's collection.*

*A diminutive table for two
and a chocolate dessert hold
center stage in this tableau.*

*This portable lunch includes
two Limoges fruit boxes.*

**Hand-painted baskets of fruits and vegetables abound in this rosy scene.**

**A picnic setting is the backdrop for these strawberry-themed boxes. The single strawberry looks like it was just picked.**

This visual garden adventure included five Limoges porcelain boxes.

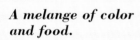

A melange of color and food.

An evocative tableau of intricately hand-painted boxes and fresh fruits and vegetables.

*Garden delights. A radish, an onion, an asparagus and an artichoke are gathered in this intriguing array.*

# CHAPTER 3
# *Fabrication*

## Clay Three Ways

Mark Twain in *A Tramp Abroad* describes his passion for ceramics and collectibles in 1879, but man's passion for ceramics goes back to Neolithic time when ceramics were first made. Ceramics is the general heading of baked clay items. Under this heading are porcelain, stoneware and earthenware.

*Porcelain:* The apex of ceramics is "hard paste" or true porcelain. True porcelain contains kaolin, the name of which is derived from the hill of Kaoling in China, where this china clay was first found. Combined with the kaolin are feldspar and quartz. This combination of components is then fired at a high (hard) temperature. If left unglazed, the product is referred to as being in the biscuit (or bisque) stage. When glazed and fired, the separate ingredients combine to form the beautiful translucent, hard, white substance which we admire today. Also referred to as porcelain, artificial or "soft paste" porcelain was initially the end product of attempts to produce a porcelain-like material. This effort was due to the lack of the key ingredient, kaolin. Soft paste porcelain was made by mixing clay, water and other compounds. In some instances what was added was a glassy compound called frit, which gave artificial porcelain its sheen. In England, starting in 1748, manufacturers added pure white bone ash products which increased the hardness of the piece. We know of these as bone porcelain. These artificial porcelain items were fired at a lower (soft) temperature than hard paste, hence the name soft paste.

*Stoneware:* Stoneware, the second division of ceramics, includes objects of clay with a high silica content. As the name implies, the product is heavy and sturdy. After baking, it fuses and does not need to be glazed to hold liquids. It was often glazed for appearance's sake. To achieve this end,

one method involved having salt shoveled into the kiln at the height of the firing. The salt set off a reaction which caused the surface to become glassy and bumpy. This product is referred to as "salt glazed" stoneware and has textured finish that some say looks like an orange peel. Stoneware is opaque; in others words, one cannot see through it.

*Earthenware:* The most basic of the three clay products is earthenware, which is porous, opaque baked clay. It is fired at a low temperature and remains porous unless glazed. Tin-glazed earthenware is known variously as *faience, maiolica* or *delft.* The glaze includes lead and tin oxides. Since it is produced and used so many countries, how it is designated varies. It is referred to as *faience* in France, Spain and Austria, *maiolica* in Italy, and *delft* in the Netherlands.

## Firing

The making of a porcelain box or other porcelain object starts long before the raw clay goes into the kiln. Initially the process begins in the creative sphere of the artist. This two-dimensional image is then transferred to reality. One method is to sculpt

***Work put into kiln by pulley or tackle block.***

# The Production Process

*Maison De La Porcelaine in Aixe Sur Vienne had a tour available.*

*First firing*

*Molds*

*Glaze bath*

*Second firing*

*The progression: raw, first fire, second fire.*

*An example of transfer/decal work.*

*Hand-painting in progress*

## Birth of a Piece

*1. Sculpture and creation of model.*

*2. After pouring and the piece is set, the molt is broken.*

*3. Hinges are customized for each piece.*

*4. Decoration gives life to the piece.*

*Adapted from Parry-Vielle Catalogue.*

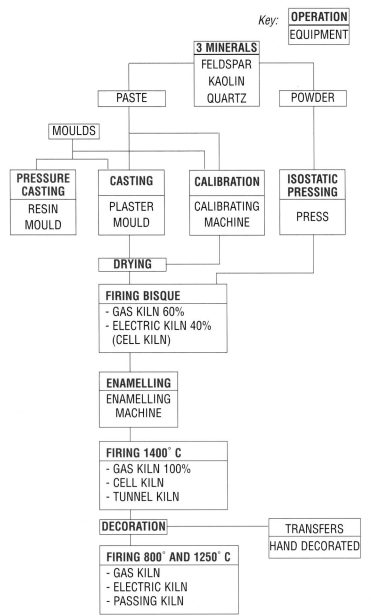

Key: 

| OPERATION |
|---|
| EQUIPMENT |

**3 MINERALS**
FELDSPAR
KAOLIN
QUARTZ

PASTE

POWDER

MOULDS

| PRESSURE CASTING | CASTING | CALIBRATION | ISOSTATIC PRESSING |
|---|---|---|---|
| RESIN MOULD | PLASTER MOULD | CALIBRATING MACHINE | PRESS |

**DRYING**

**FIRING BISQUE**
- GAS KILN 60%
- ELECTRIC KILN 40%
(CELL KILN)

**ENAMELLING**
ENAMELLING MACHINE

**FIRING 1400° C**
- GAS KILN 100%
- CELL KILN
- TUNNEL KILN

**DECORATION**

| TRANSFERS |
|---|
| HAND DECORATED |

**FIRING 800° AND 1250° C**
- GAS KILN
- ELECTRIC KILN
- PASSING KILN

## FLOW CHART

The preparation of the paste requires the combining of kaolin, feldspar and quartz.

CASTING:
For the production of hollow pieces. The slip is cast in plaster molds.

CALIBRATING:
For creating plates.

ISOSTATIC PRESSING:
For shaping flat objects.

DRYING:
Used in casting and calibrating.

FIRST FIRING-BISQUE:
This firing eliminates the residual water and destroys organic material in paste.

ENAMELLING:
Done by dipping or spraying.

FIRING AT 1400° C:
The hottest and longest firing.

DECORATION FIRING.

*Adapted from: Les Manufacturers De Porcelaine de Limoges Chambre de Commerce at Industries de Limoges et La Haute Vienne, December 1995.*

the shape out of a solid piece of plaster. A mold is made so that the shape can be reproduced. The original mold model is cut to permit the piece to be removed without distortion.

Into the mold goes liquid clay known as slip or *barbotine*. Since the molds are made of plaster, the moisture is absorbed and a clean cast can be made. A craftsman ascertains when the correct amount of moisture has been absorbed; thus leaving a layer of clay built up on the inside of the mold. The surplus slip is then disposed of and the piece is left to dry. At a certain point when the correct degree of dryness has been reached, the piece is removed from the mold. In the final step the piece dries out completely.

Heat is needed to change the raw body of clay into a hard ceramic body. In the days before temperature control, methods had to be devised to tell when pieces were done. In the time when firewood and coal were used, firing could take days. The kiln foreman had to ascertain the readiness of a piece. The color of the fire was one indicator. Another way of checking was to physically remove a sample piece to check its readiness. It has been said that a foreman could tell that the kiln was right when the heat singed his eyebrows.

Nowadays the particular item goes into an initial firing or bisque at 1100-1800° F, after which it is glazed either by submerging it in a bath or by spraying. Then the piece undergoes another firing at 2550-2900° F at which point the glaze and the body become fused, this is referred to as the glost firing. All sorts of things can go wrong at this firing stage giving rise to wasters. It is at the firing stage that these imperfections are revealed, so taking a perfectly fired piece out of the kiln is always a pleasure. When looking at a finished piece it is hard to imagine that during the entire firing process there is a 15% shrinkage rate!

## Color

Ground or main background colors on porcelain were first used in Europe by Meissen in the 1720s and were subsequently used by all the great factories. The finest ground colors were produced in France at Vincennes and Sevres around the 1750s where the colors were fused onto the soft paste porcelain to create a stunning effect. Vibrant and intense blues such as lapis lazuli and royal blue were introduced; shortly after that, a sky blue color was originated and then daffodil yellow was added. Yellow has a very narrow tolerance to firing temperatures and it is the most difficult to control in the kiln, so creating wonderful yellows was quite a feat. The striking pink associated with Madame de Pompadour was then introduced. During this time, violet was developed. The most admired color of the time was developed at Sevres. It was called celestial blue.

In addition to ground colors, intricate paintings were done in the white area or reserve. When a piece was painted using variations of just one color, it was said to be *en camaieu*. Gilded patterns, sometimes put on top of the ground colors, had wonderful names such as *oeil de perdrix* (partridge eye) or *caioutte* (crazy paving). An elaborate piece with a colored ground, detailed painting and gilding could take numerous firings and as much as 400 hours to complete.

There are two methods for firing color decorated items. The first method applies colors (metal oxides) to the biscuit stage body and firing both at the same time. This is referred to as *grand feu* or high temperature decoration. In the other method, the design is applied to the piece after the background glaze has been fired. This is known as *petit feu* or low temperature decoration. In this fashion, the piece is refired at a temperature which can be withstood by each particular oxide. Gold is applied last since it cannot withstand temperatures above 1,100 F. Since 1970, new processes have come into being which allow for firing colors at higher temperatures.

### Ceramic Turners

*This illustration shows pots or vases being made. The turner or thrower in the foreground is working with enough porcelain body to form the product. The activity takes place on a disc, which can be revolved. The person in the background is finishing off a piece.*

**129**

### Molding

*In this illustration the molder, who is in the background to the right, rolls out a sheet of porcelain, which is subsequently carried over and placed on a mold. The particular mold shown in the left foreground will produce a bowl with melon fluting. The porcelain sheet is then pressed with a sponge, forcing it to conform to the recesses of the mold (shown background-left). In the foreground to the right a craftsman "repairs" the piece.*

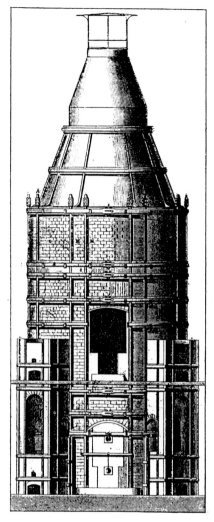

### Porcelain Kiln

### Dipping in Liquid Glazes

*Plates are placed, in the biscuit stage, into the glaze. Two craftswomen touch up the work. The first (background-left) is removing excess thickness or drops of glaze. The second woman is cleaning the foot-rim of the plate.*

# CHAPTER 4
## The Box Itself

### Boxes, Bibelots and Bijouteries

Bibelots are small art objects for personal use or decoration. Limoges boxes are bibelots that are today's representation of a style that reached its zenith around the 18th century to meet the needs of the French and other European aristocracy. These boxes of old served many purposes, from the simple concept of collecting beautiful things to the presentation by kings as gifts of gratitude. These boxes could be simple or exotic, prosaic or the height of ingenuity, given to a lover or used to solidify the friendship between nations. Boxes were one of the many unique items put into the "cabinets of the curious" at the time. Limoges produces a myriad of choices of shapes and uses for the collector of fine porcelain boxes. The following is an examination of a variety of shapes and uses of boxes, containers and bijouteries that have existed over the years, although are not exclusively made by or in Limoges.

Boxes have existed from the time the first person decided to protect his or her precious belongings or carry them to another location. Even kings used elegant boxes. According to A. Kenneth Snowman, in *18th Century Gold Boxes of Europe*, in 1471, the King of Sicily's most cherished possession was a rock crystal box. Boxes can be thought of as a window to view society. These objects allow us to experience the fashions and customs of other periods. I have chosen to group boxes and containers into 10 main categories.

### *Category One: Bibelots*

Boxes which were artistic objects for personal use or decoration span a number of categories: *etuis*, snuff boxes, *tabatieres*, *bonbonnieres*, patch boxes and presentation boxes. In addition these numerous boxes had variations within them.

First is the *etui*, which translates to case or sheath in French. In other words, it is the name used for very small boxes. Many things fall under this heading. Small boxes were made to hold items for use such as: manicuring sets, tweezers, sewing equipment, snuff spoons, compasses, scent bottles, writing or drawing implements. They could be many shapes: cylindrical, flattened, rectangular or conforming to the object it surrounded. Some were done in sculptural forms such as a stockinged woman's leg.

*Etuis* were made of many different materials: gold, silver, porcelain, painted enamel, etc. An *etui* could be carried in the pocket or worn hanging on a *chatelaine*.

One *etui* of particular interest is the *souvenir*—a small *etui* whose name derives from the French word meaning memory, memorandum book or case. The Louvre uses the designation, *etui a tablettes* or *etui-souvenir*. This box is a flat, rectangular container with a hinged lid. The interior is fitted with one or more ivory leaves, *tablettes,* for notes and a pencil. The term derives from the inscription *Souvenir/d'Amitie* on the box. The *souvenir* was used for domestic purposes, such as writing down appointments. Madame de Pompadour was known to have had eight *souvenirs.*

**Carnets de bal:** The *carnet de bal* (French for dance notebook) is similar in appearance. It was a beautifully decorated container enclosing pages or an ivory slate, with an accompanying pencil. Ladies used it to list the names of their dance partners. Whereas the *souvenir* was for domestic use, the *carnet de bal* was specifically a dance card. Both were filled with ivory tablets, whose guild, *tabletiers,* had existed since the 13th century.

**Necessaires**: The *necessaire* was a small writing or personal item accessory case, fashionable throughout Europe in the 18th century. It is thought by some that the distinction between a *necessaire* and *etui* is that a *necessaire* is partitioned and an *etui* is hollow. However, the designations *etui* and *necessaire* are often used interchangeably.

**Snuff boxes:** The snuff box or *tabatiere* (French for snuff box) is the next category: Snuff boxes were containers to hold snuff (powdered tobacco which was taken by sniffing into the nostril). What is considered to be the first snuff box was a container in the shape of a pear, with a hole on the top, which would allow the snuff to be poured out. Pocket snuff boxes were for personal use and needed to be small enough to fit in one's pocket or other small repository. They varied in size but usually were about 2-3 inches wide. With 18th century royalty's prevailing interest in finery, pocket snuff boxes served as a wonderful vehicle for showcasing masterpieces of artistry. They were usually hinged, although some had sliding or screw tops. An interesting example of the sliding top snuff box is one on which the lid twists around to disclose an open area, just the perfect size to pinch out the snuff, after which the box can be slid shut. Snuff boxes needed to have hinged or easily opened lids, since the procedure for taking snuff and keeping the snuff in the box required one free hand.

The hinged lid made for a tight closure which was also important since the lid had to be secure or the snuff would become loose in one's pocket or get damp. The most expensive boxes were mounted in gold or silver; others were mounted with copper or other less expensive metals. When the gold or silver enclosed the corners of the box, it was referred to as *en cage*. This was helpful in times when the use of gold was restricted to a certain weight. In addition to the common rectangular, oval or round shapes, they could be cartouche- or bombe-shaped or made of a mixture of materials.

The list of materials that pocket snuff boxes were made of, or with, is extensive. In addition to molded porcelain, there were porcelain plaques, miniature paintings, vernis Martin, ivory, Japanese lacquer, *pietra-dura,* micromosaics, ancient artifacts mounted on boxes and an interesting sign of the times, the *tabatiere a la Silhouette.* These boxes took their name from the French Minister of Finance under Louis XV, Etienne de Silhouette. The silhouette was usually the center motif. The use of the name Silhouette in this connection has had a number of interpretations, one being that cut out pictures were a cheap form of portraiture and

he was viewed as ungenerous. Another way that the top of a box could be formed was by "harnessing." In this technique the gold or silver was entwined throughout the lid, being incorporated into the design. This was done extensively with hardstones.

With time and invention, perfumed and flavored snuff were introduced. The double, triple, quadruple or even quintuple sectioned box was one of the outcomes of the use of perfumed snuff; some compartments being for scented (or flavored) snuff and others for regular snuff. The thumb snuff box was an interesting sub-category of the double box. This box was worn on the thumb, with the thumb fitting into the hole at the center. The box could be easily carried, affording the owner the opportunity to offer snuff to the left and right simultaneously. The box could be used for perfumed or regular snuff.

The puzzle snuff box was another interesting division of snuff boxes. These boxes had involved opening devices which had to be manipulated in a particular order to open or close. Since an interesting snuff box was something to be desired, a number of variations existed which required a second look or offered a surprise. Mechanism or automaton boxes fell under this heading. They were boxes that on initial viewing would appear to be normal lidded boxes. However, these boxes on closer inspection (or with manipulation) would reveal different mechanisms. These would fall into the category of automata. Included in this array of movement were miniature action scenes, watches or music boxes. Another box of interest is the *tabatiere a secret*; this box had a central motif that, when a specific spot was pressed, would open to reveal a miniature portrait that had been hidden underneath. Boxes were also made with false bottoms or double lids.

The singing bird snuff box was the apex of snuff box production. These boxes were the consummation of the combined efforts of watchmakers, goldsmiths and jewelers. This impressive creation was manufactured in such a way that when one pressed a button (or lever) the top central portion of the cover opened and revealed a mechanical "singing" little canary (*serinette*), which sang for a short time and then, was gone. The bird, about half an inch, could be brightly colored and would contain a mechanism which made the head and beak move, the wings flutter and the bird change position. The mechanism for producing the song was generated by a bellows. Over time, less expensive copies have been made. Words do not express fully how wonderful these are. When I saw one at an antique show, people flocked around to see it. The quality of the craftsmanship and the small scale were incredible.

The shape of a porcelain box constitutes another category. Snuff boxes and *bonbonnieres* (small containers for sweetmeats) were called "fantasies" or "fantasy boxes" when they were made in an unusual, sculptural shape. These shapes might depict such things as animals, barrels, hats, chairs, trunks, shells, etc. They were considered to be for pocket use. There is one snuff box with an unusual shape from a later date that requires mention: the *tabatiere au petit-chapeau*, this snuff box was made in the shape of Napoleon's hat. The use of this snuff box was an indicator of one's loyalty to Napoleon.

An interesting snuff box exists for which the shape and size are related to the activity in which it was used. It was the *tabatiere de chasse*. This snuff box was made to use while engaged in the royal custom of the hunt, specifically with enough snuff for the activity. This box could be decorated with a hunting scene. As was the custom, the box would coordinate with the riding costume. In addition to the *tabatiere de chasse* being coordinated, other outfits were matched. If one's outfit was light-colored it would follow that the box would be in concert. In winter it was fashionable to have a box with a snow scene. Season, weight of fabric, activi-

ty and color were all factors in choosing the snuff box to wear on a particular day.

Some pocket snuff boxes were multi-purpose and might be made to include in its design a music box, scent bottle or sealing stamp. A pocket snuff box had to easily fit into a pocket. If it was too large, it then fit into the category of table snuff box.

The table snuff box was larger than about 4 inches, as this would indicate that it was too large for the pocket. Table boxes or mantle boxes were large boxes used in the home. The table box was utilized in a social setting and passed around so snuff taking could be enjoyed while drinking wine. Mantle boxes were kept on fireplace mantles for the enjoyment of visitors.

**Containers for sweets**: Another delightful box for personal use was the "sweetmeats" box. Sweets were referred to by different terms over time. A broad term used beginning in the 15th century was sweetmeats, which included items made with sugar. The *drageoir* was a container for *dragees*, a particular sweet; the term *drageoir* was used prior to 1770. The *bonbonniere* was also a container for sweets; being derived from *bonbon* the French word meaning sweetmeat. The term sweetmeat included candied fruit, sugar-coated nuts and seeds or similar sweet delicacies. The name *bonbonniere* sounds appealing but in reality people used aromatic sweets to some extent to make up for poor dental hygiene and bad breath. To offer sweets from a *bonbonniere*, the box was turned upside down and the lid was then on top.

Some of these boxes were deeply concave and came in elaborate shapes: animals, heads of ani-

*Plate # 15, bonbonniere with reclining woman, 3-1/4" long, 2-1/4" wide, 2-1/2" high. Mark: Chamart France (Charles Martine) ca.1960s.*

*Plate # 18, bonbonniere of cat with pewter base, 3-1/2" long, 2-3/8" wide, 2-1/2" high. Mark: Chanill (Chanille) 1980s-1990s.*

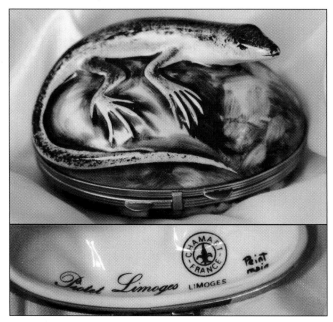

*Plate #16, bonbonniere with lizard, 3-1/4" long, 2-1/4" wide, 1-7/8" high. Mark: Chamart (Charles Martine) ca.1960s.*

mals or humans, fruits, vegetables, flowers, shells, musical instruments, art equipment, etc. These unusual shapes were sometimes referred to as "fantasies." An aligned but larger box is the *comfit* box (or *cumfitt* box). *Comfit* boxes were used as early as 1490 to hold *comfits*, tiny strongly scented sweets. These breath fresheners were made with items such as caraway, coriander or aniseed. (Shakespeare referred to them as kissing *comfits*.) *Comfit* holders, a variation on this theme, were *comfit* containers incorporated with a porcelain figure. These containers, usually in pairs, were readily available at formal and informal gatherings for the indulgence of guests, who used them after smoking or drinking. It is said that Louis XIV kept a *drageoir* with aniseed close at hand to cover his bad breath.

**Patch boxes:** The patch box or *boite a mouche* deserves special consideration. These boxes were used by the aristocracy to hold silk, thin leather or taffeta patches which were adornments for the face and body. The patch which was used beginning in the 16th century could be circular, geometric or in imaginative shapes such as stars, different phases of the moon or more ostentatious shapes such as one mentioned that was in the shape of a coach and six horses. Patch boxes held these adornments (although the one with coach and horses was probably applied at home) and might also contain a steel mirror in the lid (or a glass mirror after 1785) or a brush and adhesive to attach the patch. They were similar to snuff boxes in shape (circular, oval or oblong) but not as deep. Some had areas for complimentary cosmetics, such as kohl, for use as an eye liner and rouge. These combination boxes were used by men and women, since men also used enhancers. Patch boxes went out of style in the 19th century.

**Portrait boxes:** Sometimes the *boite a portrait*, which literally translates to portrait box, was referred to as a snuff box. This box contained a miniature portrait, painted or enameled, on the cover or inside. It was mentioned by authorities that the use of the term in relation to boxes was begun as a device to circumvent King Louis XIV's dislike of snuff. A *boite a portrait* had previously referred to a holder for a miniature portrait and had not been banned by Louis. Initially the portraits were placed on the inside of the box, but later were mounted on the outside to prevent contact with the tobacco. These delightful boxes so pleased Louis that he gave them as gifts. When used by kings, these boxes were predominantly made of gold and were magnificent masterworks. One particularly impressive gold portrait box was given to Benjamin Franklin in recognition of his position as minister to the Court of Louis XVI. The diamonds on it surrounded the portrait and bordered the box. In an alternate usage, the *boite a portrait* referred to a shallow portrait box that could be used to hold a precious memento. The term at different points was used interchangeably with *tabatiere* or snuff box. Sometimes it was referred to as "*tabatiere a portrait.*"

**Boites diplomatique:** Whether called *boite a portrait*, snuff box or presentation box, these boxes became the expected or mandatory gift at the completion of a mission, momentous event or term of office. Another box name associated with the commission of an important activity was the *boite diplomatique*. This box was given to diplomats at the time of important treaties. The importance of the event or person was indicated by the magnificence of the box. To underscore the strength of this custom, we see the practice of giving the box to the widow of an official intended as the recipient. In an alternate usage the presentation box served as a tactful emissary. If a box was presented to a king as a diplomatic gesture and it was accepted, that boded well for the future.

**Freedom boxes:** The freedom box is a special type of presentation box. Although its use was in the 18th century, it is similar in concept to the keys to the city, in use in the 20th century. The gold freedom box was given accompanied by some pomp and ceremony. The box had the arms of the city engraved on the lid to commemorate the event. In addition to this, it could have a scroll enclosed commemorating the city and the event. The message of thanks was well understood.

**Message boxes:** There were other types of message boxes, the first being the *boite a message*. These were locked metal boxes, sometimes silver, for secret correspondence. They date from the late 14th century. Another type of box referred to as a message box was one that had printed messages on the surface; they might have printed adages or references to places visited. The possible themes expressed could be about daily life or diversions from it. They could refer to relationships, politics, the theater or current events. A very specialized box that fits in this category is the calendar box. This was a snuff box where the outside of the box served as a calendar.

Boxes within the heading of event boxes would be the ballooning or Montgolfier box. Snuff boxes, *tabatieres au ballon* and other desirable objects were decorated with ballooning motifs to commemorate the ballooning attempts that were taking place in France. Jacques Etienne and Joseph Michel Montgolfier's successful manned venture in 1783 caused quite a stir.

Another box related to secrets is the *boite a secret*. At first viewing, the box looked like it was covered with agate. Upon bringing it near heat, a picture was revealed. When removed from the warm area, such as near a fireplace, it returned to its original state. The secret was a sealed layer of wax, which dissolved or solidified depending on the temperature.

## Category Two:

## Food-Related Boxes or Containers

**Shallow handled containers:** The *ecuelle* is a shallow two-handled bowl which could be with or without a cover. It is said to be peculiar to France and was used beginning in the 17th century. Sometimes it was included in leather traveling cases along with a dish, knife, spoon and fork. The *ecuelle* was frequently used for women late in pregnancy or early after childbirth, as it was easy to use. Limoges porcelain examples exist from the 18th century (at the Adrien Dubouche Museum).

The caudle cup is also a two-handled porcelain or pottery container which could be with or without a cover. It was used in the 18th century for caudle, a thin gruel mixed with spiced wine or ale and possibly bread or oatmeal. The shapes varied and could be round, straight sided or shallow. This superseded spout cups, such as the posset pot.

The posset pot was a handled lidded container with a spout, used for posset in the 17th century. Posset was a popular drink made with hot ale, milk, sugar and spices (and possibly small pieces of bread, toast or oatcake) or in another version, spiced cream and wine. Another handled shallow container was the porringer which was for porridge, broth or semi-liquid food. The distinctive feature of the porringer was the tab-like handle(s). The difference in these containers at first was an enigma to me, but upon closer inspection the major difference, I find, has to do with the food served in it, although the posset pot is set apart by having a spout.

**Spice boxes:** Spices were very important in cooking as they offset the less appealing aspects of preserved meats. Spice boxes came in many manifestations. Different containers have been referred to as spice boxes or casters over time. In the Middle Ages, spices were readily available in India and China. Shipping to Europe and the incumbent taxation brought about exorbitant prices. Therefore, spices were precious and were often kept in locked cases. One later variation of the

*Plate #27, porringer with exquisite detail work. 4-3/4" diameter on plate, 3-1/2" from edge of cup to edge of tab. Mark: G. D. & Co (Gustave Demartial) ca. 1880-1890.*

spice box included a small hinged box with a tiny ladle. Another small hinged oval spice box was made with pinch-sides. To open this box, the widest part of the box was pressed, which resulted in the box springing open. Still another variation was a box with a shell outline and scalloped lid. However, the broadest category of spice box was a plain box that held spices with the possibility of different purposes. In the 18th century, a variation was the double spice box, which had a lid which was hinged in the center. The two sides of the box could be hollow or one side could contain a nutmeg grater. Another term used in relation to spice containers was spice caster.

**Caster:** The caster (or castor) was a small container, originally popular in the 18th century, for casting salt, sugar or other spices. It was usually cylindrical and had a perforated domed top. Casters could range from plain and utilitarian to very elaborate. A variation of these was the muffineer which was used specifically for cinnamon in conjunction with muffins, and baked wheat cakes. The term originated in the 19th century but the use predated that time, starting in the 18th century. Casters were made in many materials including silver, porcelain and pottery.

**Mustard pots:** The mustard pot was used beginning in the 18th century; it was a container for holding condiments, particularly mustard. A telling characteristic is the indentation or space to allow for a serving device or spoon. The mustard pot was preceded in use by the unpierced caster (or pierced caster with a sleeve), mustard at that point being stored dry and mixed on a plate.

**Nutmeg graters:** The nutmeg grater was a popular accouterment. This was a pocket-sized box with a metal grating area for pulverizing nutmeg, which was used to enhance the taste of wine, ale or hot toddy (rum) drinks and custards. Nutmeg was thought to be a stimulant which could purify breath and help reduce flatulence. Tavern keepers did not necessarily supply nutmeg in drinks and did not want to place nutmeg graters on the table for fear of the nutmeg and grater being stolen. Therefore it became fashionable to carry a pocket nutmeg grater. They came in silver, ivory, wood and other materials, in many different shapes including a keg shape which alluded to its use for spicing hot toddies.

**Salt containers:** These containers also underwent numerous metamorphoses. From the 14th century to the early 17th century, before salt deposits were found, salt was a precious and prized commodity. It was even used as a form of payment. At that time, the salt container could be over a foot tall and decorated with gems and was referred to as a "standing salt." (Salt was initially obtained from plants, saline streams and ocean water.) An outstanding standing salt, dating from the 16th century, made of gilded silver and inset with Limoges enamel plaques is on display at the Wallace Collection in London. The placement of the salt container was an indicator of social standing. If one sat "above" the salt at the table one knew they had greater status. Being seated "below" the salt showed a lower rank.

*Plate #26, mustard pot with pink roses. Signed. Mark: P. P. (Paroutaud Freres/La Seynie) ca.1900-1920. (Courtesy of Susan Wolf)*

*Plate #29, salt cellar with violets. Mark: GDA (Gerard, Dufraisseix and Abbot) ca. 1900 to 1930. (Courtesy of Chris Christensen)*

The 18th century set the stage for some extraordinary figural salt holders. A pair of beautifully decorated reclining figures holding salt bowls, is shown in Allan and Helen Smith's, *1334 Open Salts Illustrated, The Tenth Book* (see plate #452 in their book). When salt became affordable, it was served at the table in "salts" or "open salts," which were placed beside each plate or within the use of several people. This container could be made of silver, porcelain, ceramic, wood or glass. The terminology for salt containers varied with time and location. So names such as salt cellar, salt trencher, salt dip and salt cup could be used interchangeably. The term "salt" or "open salt" is used to differentiate the container from the salt shaker, which has a lid. The salt shaker came into use in the late-1800s.

A utilitarian manifestation of the salt container is the salt box. To keep salt readily accessible, this container was hung on the wall. In the late 1700s, these salt boxes were in common usage in kitchens and were kept on the wall near the cooking area to keep the salt available and dry.

**Sugar boxes:** Starting in the 16th century, the sugar box was used as an accessory for wine drinking. Its purpose was to make inexpensive wine more palatable. A variation of this was the double-lidded box, one side of which held refined white sugar and the other ambered sugar (mixed with ambergris and musk) to reduce the roughness of the wine.

**Sauce tureens:** The sauce tureen, a smaller version of the soup tureen, was made in matched sets to go with the tableware. Sauces began as a remedy or disguise for the taste of preserved foods. Initially they were put in a saucer, "a small dish to hold sauce." After the saucer/dish, came the sauce

boat in the 17th century and the sauce tureen in the 18th. They could be silver, porcelain or pottery.

**Tea, Coffee, and Chocolate Containers:** Tea, along with coffee and chocolate, had become available in Europe in the 17th century. By the 18th century, these exotic drinks had provided the wealthy with another avenue for porcelain use and self-indulgence. Manufacturers provided the necessary trappings. Tea was initially an expensive item and was used judiciously. Tea was stored and sometimes served from containers referred to as: tea canisters, tea bottles or tea caddies. The name "caddy" was derived from the term "kati" (a Malay word), the standard weight for a package of tea. The equivalent English weight was about 1-1/3 pounds. Tea containers had tightly fitted lids and

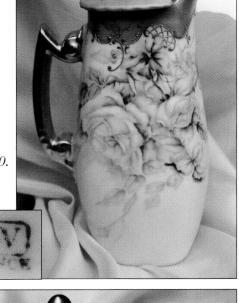

*Plate #25, chocolate pot with yellow roses. 9" high, 5" greatest width including handle. Mark: T & V (Tressemanes & Vogt) ca. 1890-1910.*

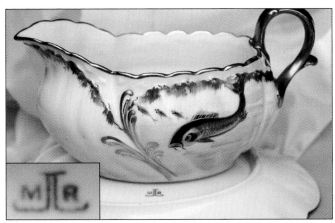

*Plate #28, sauce boat with fish scene. 8-3/4" long, 6" wide on plate. 7-1/4" long, 3-1/4" wide on boat. Mark: MR (Martial Redon & Co.) Ca. 1880 to 1890.*

*Plate #22, sugar holder with yellow and pink roses. 4" diameter, 3-7/8" high mark: PL (La Porcelaine Limousine) ca.1900-1930s.*

*Plate #23, marabout (small hot water pitcher) or individual server with gilded handle, spout and lid handle. 5-1/4" high, 3" diameter at base.*
*Marks: banner and bird (Charles Martin), triangle (Charles Martin & Duche) ca.1900-1930.*

were sometimes locked. During the 18th century one could see a tea chest or trunk, a lined or partitioned wooden box (resembling luggage and hence the name) for storing caddies or canisters. It could include an assemblage of two or three containers. If three containers were included, the center one held sugar. A tea trunk could be covered with leather or shagreen.

Time passed, customs changed, and it became fashionable to serve tea differently. Matching porcelain tea serving sets came into vogue, and they could include (in addition to cups, saucers, teapots, and trays) sugar containers, creamers and a porcelain lidded containers for storing or serving the dry tea leaves. Coffee and hot chocolate drinks were also very popular. Porcelain coffee and chocolate pots and their respective serving sets were in demand. An interesting looking porcelain drink-related item also available is the *marabout*, a small hot water pitcher with a lid and a stick-like handle.

**Veilleuses:** Truly in a category of its own is the *veilleuse*. Its name comes from the French verb *veiller*, meaning to keep a night vigil. It was originally a night lamp which evolved into a food or tea warmer with an *ecuelle* or teapot, to be kept at bedside. Made of porcelain or pottery it was also used for posset and caudle. It was made with a hollow pedestal base with a hole for a small source of heat. (The heating lamp was referred to as a *godet*, a small receptacle containing oil and a wick.) In some instances, it had a double boiler portion, filled with water. One elaborate form of the *veilleuse* was called a *personage* and took the form of a costumed individual. The *veilleuse* was also made in an architectural form, a beautiful example being a Gothic cathedral made of Limoges porcelain which is on display at the Adrien Dubouche Museum.

**Liquor holders:** If one wanted to store liquor, there were wooden decanter boxes, which held four to six square decanters and possibly a few drinking glasses. A tantalizing liquid-related item is the *tantalus*. This unusual case held three decanters or perfume containers which allowed one to see the decanters but not use them unless the case was unlocked. A flat bar or collar restricted the bottles. It was named after *Tantalus*, from Greek mythology, the king of Phrygia who could see food and water but not partake.

**Viand-shaped containers:** Viand-shaped or related containers were continuously popular. Tureens, terrines, vessels, jugs, covered dishes or other containers in the shape of animals, fruits or vegetables were produced in porcelain and pottery in 18th century Europe. They included containers such as:

1) Large serving tureens with game birds on the cover

2) Covered terrines decorated with a goose or game bird in bas relief

3) Small tureens in the shape of pumpkins, pomegranates, melons (with melon fluting), etc.

4) Jugs or containers in the shape of artichokes, cabbage, cauliflower or lettuce

5) Jam pots (*confituriers*) in the shape of different fruits (such as oranges, figs, apples or pears).

**Zoomorphic boxes:** Zoomorphic imagery boxes, in which animals were represented on decorative porcelain boxes, began in the 18th century in soft paste. Animals were represented in other containers such as life-sized ceramic sitting hens, which were used as the vehicle for serving the enclosed boiled eggs, in their egg cups.

**Supplemental dishes:** Elaborate dinner services in the 18th century required some supple-

*Plate #24, covered butter with gilded handle and accents. 6-7/8" diameter of plate, 5-3/8" diameter of dome cover. Marks: B & Cie (Balleroy et Cie), torch in circle (Flambeau China) 1910-1930.*

mental dishes one might not expect today. Covered containers for butter such as the butter tub, dish or box, were used beginning as early as the 1500s. These containers could be made of porcelain, pottery or silver, and their lid or sides sometimes were decorated with dairy motifs.

**Chestnut baskets:** The chestnut basket from the 18th century developed into a ceramic basket with an openwork, flower encrusted lid. It was sometimes accompanied with a stand. The body of the basket could be covered with flowers in varying degrees of relief. Hot roasted (unpeeled) chestnuts were served in these, to be peeled and eaten accompanied by coffee. Used in the 18th and 19th centuries, incredible (covered) open work baskets were manufactured by Belleek in the 1860s. These were made of thin porcelain ropes layered to form a basket. The basket was then finished with full relief flowers.

**Cutlery boxes:** Utilitarian objects are necessary for everyday life and resourcefulness resulted in the cutlery box. These boxes were hung on the wall in the kitchen and held knives and forks. These wooden boxes were tapered at the bottom and had a hinged top. A wonderfully innovative idea in storage for special occasions is represented by the knife box. These containers were made to hold knives, forks and spoons, vertically, so that the theft of cutlery would be noticed. These partitioned containers were made starting in the 16th century. Knife boxes often had a distinctive bowed front and sloped top. An interesting 18th century manifestation of this was done in the classical urn shape. Knife boxes fell out of fashion in the early 19th century, when cutlery drawers were built into sideboards.

## Category Three:
### Writing Boxes and Containers

**Ink-related containers:** Before the ubiquitous ball-point pen came into being, many items were necessary or desired for the well appointed writing experience. An absolute necessity was the inkwell or inkpot. A container for ink, into which a pen or quill could be dipped, was made in porcelain starting in the 18th century. There is some dispute about the next item. The pounce box, according to some authorities, contained something called pounce powder, which was used to prevent ink from spreading. The pounce powder per these authorities was made of gum sandarac (the powdered resin from a Northwest African tree). There is another school on this, and they make reference to the idea of pounce relating to having perforations.

**Sealing and stamp boxes:** In times gone by, people were desirous of sealing the back of their letters with a special wafer. Small boxes to contain these wafers were made from the 16th to mid 19th century. They were made of porcelain, silver or glass. The "wafer" was made of a dried paste (of flour or gelatin) and some coloring. In the 19th century, the stamp box seems to have replaced it. The stamp box had an interesting configuration; it had a sloping bottom which made the removal of the stamps easier. If one was writing at home at a desk, an inkstand to organize and store writing equipment was available. Inkstands were made in many materials. An incredibly appealing 19th century inkstand or *encrier* is displayed at the Adrien Dubouche Museum. It was made by Baignol and its central motif is a cherub.

**Writing boxes:** If one were traveling, writing equipment was made available by use of a writing box or case. This term was used from the 17th century to describe a box or case which held writing implements which could include some of the following: ink, inkpot, pounce(t) pot, wafer box, seal, paper, pencil, pens or eraser. The writing box could be made in different materials. The boxes sometimes measured less than 3 inches long…quite a feat!

## Category Four:
### Needlework Boxes and Containers

**Bodkin cases:** It's odd to find a bodkin nowadays, but bodkin cases are still around. A bodkin case was a tubular-shaped box with a slip-on lid and rounded ends, which was used in the 18th century to hold special needles. Bodkins (the term being in use in the 16th century) were large-eyed needles whose specialized use was to draw a string or ribbon through a loop formed by fabric at the neck, waist, wrist or hem of a garment. The outcome desired was that clothes would remain in place until one opened the tie to undress. Bodkins therefore needed to be carried since repairs or rethreadings were necessary on the numerous tying devices. A bodkin or bodkins set could be given as a gift and might be silver engraved and monogrammed.

**Thimble cases:** Another sewing accessory was the thimble case. It was a small container and could mimic the thimble shape or be larger. Thimble cases were made of a variety of materials, including porcelain.

**Needlework boxes:** The needlework box or case for needlework came in many guises over time. Since early pins and needles were individually handmade and scarce, special care was taken with them. To avoid loss or pilferage, they were not left at home but were carried when traveling in a case, e.g. *etui*, pouch, etc. Time passed and by the 18th century, the needlework box became a fitted box to hold needles, threads and tools for both practical and decorative sewing needs. An aligned but smaller object was the sewing case.

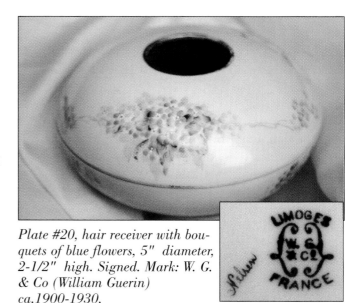

*Plate #20, hair receiver with bouquets of blue flowers, 5" diameter, 2-1/2" high. Signed. Mark: W. G. & Co (William Guerin) ca.1900-1930.*

ous times: powder boxes, scent bottles, pomade pots, jewel boxes, and ring stands. The 18th century set could consist of a porcelain tray laden with candlesticks, a brush and comb (possible porcelain handle), powder boxes and subsidiary porcelain boxes for additional needs. One interesting item sometimes found included on the vanity tray was the hair receiver. This was a covered box with a hole in the center. This receptacle received the combings which were eventually used to supplement the current hairstyle. Rouge or eye shadow boxes could be found in the extensive porcelain

## Category Five:

### Vanity-related Containers

**Vanity sets:** Boxes to hold face or body powder were known as early as 1380. By necessity, they are larger than snuff boxes. Vanity sets (*garniture de toilette*) for the dressing table, were made in porcelain and included at vari-

*Plate #35, hair receiver 4-1/4" diameter and puff box 4-1/8" diameter, with pink roses. Signed. Mark: T & V rectangle ca. 1892 to 1907. (Courtesy of Dorothy Kamm)*

*Plate #36, four piece dresser set (including hair receiver, puff box, hat pin holder and candlestick), with chickory design, 4-1/4" diameter. Mark: W.G. & Co. Ca. 1900 to 1915. (Courtesy of Dorothy Kamm)*

*Plate #6, pomade container with pink cherry blossoms, 1-1/2" diameter, 1-3/4" high. Mark: W. G. & Co (William Guerin) ca. After 1900-1930.*

vanity sets that were made.

**Compacts:** Another container used from the late 19th century to the present, is the compact. It is sometimes referred to as a "Dorine Case," based on the name of the French manufacturer of cosmetics and cases.

**Perfume containers:** Perfume or scents could be contained in numerous cases. The perfume box was a receptacle containing a glass perfume bottle (sometimes with a lock). Scent bottles were distinctive containers for perfume which came in many shapes, including the shape of a human or animal. In figural scent bottles, the head often served as the perfume stopper. Scent bottles could be glass with a porcelain exterior but were also made of materials other than porcelain.

Sometimes the bottles were double-ended with one side for smelling salts and the other for perfume. Scents were used in two ways: as an ally in seduction or to mask offending body odors. By the early 19th century cleanliness started to become important.

**Jewelry holders:** Upon finishing one's toilette, it was time to put on the jewelry. A jewelry case or casket is a small box for jewelry; some of these boxes were on stands. The word "casket" was used from 1878 until the early 1900s. Another container related to attending to one's toilette is the compendium or fitted casket. These boxes were made starting in the 17th century and featured little drawers and fitted areas for storing vanity and personal care items.

And now with the preparation finished, it's time to go…traveling.

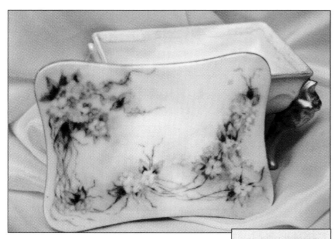

*Plate #2, jewelry casket with forget me nots and ribbons, 4-1/8" long, 3" wide, 2-7/16" high. Mark: ADK (A. Klingenberg) ca. 1890-1910.*

## Category Six: Traveling Boxes

**Traveling cases:** Coach travel brought about different demands and particular containers met the challenge. A canteen or traveling case was used in the 17th and 18th centuries. Often covered with shagreen, it contained a silver knife, fork and spoon with a cup and possibly a condiment box and other accessories. Other containers were used for coach travel. Compendium, campaign set or ladies' companion were some of the names given to these helpful cases. The case might contain any of the items needed for a journey, which could include sewing tools, jars and bottles for cosmetic items, candlesticks, drinking cups, writing equipment, jewelry and a mirror. Some contained areas for secreting away valuables.

**Card cases:** In England, beginning in 18th century and continuing until telephone use obviated the need, one carried a card case, for this was the time when the custom of calling and leaving a card was practiced. These items were lavished with detail and produced in a broad range of materials. They were slightly larger than the standard calling card, about 4 inches long and 3 inches wide.

## Category Seven: Diversions

**Diversions:** Boxes with musical movements were developed in the 18th century. Music boxes were associated with the clock-making industry. A variation on this theme is the "music box" surmounted with a (pseudo) caged bird. Games or game accessories were sometimes enclosed in containers, e.g., chess, dice or dominoes. Game-related accessories ranged from simple to elaborate. A simple counter box for games would be a cylindrical case with a removable lid. Going to the elaborate, in the Metropolitan Museum's Linsky Collection, there is a gaming set, which consists of a finely painted enamel box enclosing enameled counter pieces.

## Category Eight: Beautification of the Home (or Castle)

**Perfuming devices:** Containers in the home included the *cassolette* (a covered vase with a perforated lid, which contained perfume); the pastille burner (a covered container with a vent, which could hold a smoldering scented pastille); and the perfume burner or *brule parfum* (a container with a pierced cover and terminating with a heating device underneath to facilitate the permeation of perfume). These containers were used beginning in the 16th century to perfume rooms. The use of perfume was important since ventilation was inadequate and personal hygiene was poor. The lack of cleanliness was due, in part, to the generally held belief that water injured the skin. People, including ladies and gentlemen of the Court, rarely washed!

**Pastille burners:** In England in the 18th and 19th centuries, a variation of the pastille burner was the cottage pastille burner, which was used due to continuing conditions of poor ventilation and cleanliness. These were made in the shape of buildings, such as Tudor cottages, Medieval castles, mills, etc. They could be decorated with faux grass, water, etc. The pastille burner had either an opening in the back, a separate base or a lift-off roof to allow for the insertion of the pastille. The chimney would release the scented fumes. Sometimes produced in the same mold shape as pastille burners was the pottery money box. In the back of the pottery house, was a slot for depositing the coin.

***Pot pourri* containers:** *Pot pourri* containers were another vehicle for scenting the environment. *Pot pourri* in French literally means "rotten pot." The name is derived from the method for preparing *pot pourri*, which consisted of layering dried flowers (flower petals, roots, seeds and leaves), bark and spices with salt to meld them. This produced a pungent, enduring scent. Houses were not well-ventilated and sanitation was neglected, so methods were used to mask the smells, giving rise to *pot pourri* and other perfuming devices and their containers. A wonderful rare example of a porcelain *pot pourri* container (which is also a table centerpiece) is available for viewing at either the Getty Museum in Los Angeles or the Wallace Collection in London. It is referred to as *vaisseau a mat* or ship with a mast. This *pot pourri* container/table centerpiece is in the form of a ship with rigging and sail and has a mast with a banner draping down the side. The banner is sprinkled with *fleur-de-lys*. The form of this container has interest in an additional aspect; the single mast ship is a symbol on the coat of arms of Paris.

***Garnitures de cheminee:*** Truly an elegant way to beautify one's environment was to decorate the mantel with a series of covered and uncovered vases, which were called *garniture de cheminee*. This suite of objects consisted of up to seven pieces. It contained a central covered vase flanked by the other vases.

**Bougie boxes:** Boxes were also used for lighting. In the 18th century the *bougie* box was used. *Bougie* was the French word for a wax candle. The box was small, cylindrical and contained a coiled wax taper, the end of which emerged through a hole in the lid of the box. This box afforded one a readily available supply of candle.

**Lithophanes:** Lithophanes are a wonderful visual addition. The name comes from the Greek, *lithos* meaning stone and *phane* meaning light. Lithophanes are scenes on flat surfaces or votives which become more visible with a back light. The bisque porcelain surface is made up of various thicknesses in the form of an intaglio. The process was invented in 1827 by M.P. de Bourgoing and introduced the following year. Lithophanes took the form of night lights, pictures, etc. They were recently re-introduced in Limoges porcelain.

## *Category Nine: Containers For Medicinal Items*

**Pomanders:** The pomander was a container worn as jewelry by people from the Middle Ages to the 17th century to prevent illness and mask odors. It was the precursor to the *vinaigrette*. They were usually round, some being compartmentalized with the divisions possibly containing different spices and/or perfumes. When the ball was opened it looked like orange segments falling from a dowel. The pomander evolved into purely decorative jewelry.

***Pounce(t)* boxes:** The pounce(t) box, a small container with a perforated lid, comes historically between the pomander and the *vinaigrette* in the mid-16th century; as with the pomander and *vinaigrette* it was used to ward off malevolent things and sweeten the air.

***Vinaigrettes:*** In the 18th century more potent vinegar facilitated the change to the *vinaigrette*. The *vinaigrette* was a small container from the 17th through the mid-19th century which often had a hinged grid to hold a sponge soaked with vinegar or perfume in place. Aromatic vinegar was thought to prevent infection, be of assistance in times of fainting and megrims (headaches or doldrums), and also covered odors. People wore or carried these containers. In addition to vinegar, people sometimes added scents of mint, cinnamon, lavender, roses, oranges or spices. Although the name is French, it is actually an English invention, with the French calling it, *boite de perfum*. *Vinaigrettes* came in many shapes including: books, baskets, purses and animals which included the unusual form of a jointed fish. With passing time they became decorative items and were given as a token of affection.

## Category Ten:

## Tobacco Boxes and Containers

**Snuff mulls:** The Scottish snuff mull, although originally not containing tobacco, was part of the history of snuff taking in Scotland. The snuff mull, was comprised of a small curved horn with a hinged lid. The lid could be quite elaborate; sometimes a local stone, Cairngorm, was used in the design. The mull was employed in the late 16th century for among other things, "naughty breath." A form of powdered yarrow was used, known as "sneeshin" and to take a pinch of snuff was "sneesing." These containers were made from the horn of the ram, cow or goat. The inside of the horn was sometimes rough cut to provide a surface for grinding the tobacco. Snuff mulls were sometimes accompanied by tools for use such as: a hare's foot

*Plate #21, tobacco jar with image of turn of the century woman lighting a cigarette, 5-1/2" diameter, 5-1/4" high. Mark: GDA (Gerard, Dufraisseix and Abbot) ca. 1900-1920.*

for wiping snuff from the upper lip or mustache, a small hammer for breaking up clumped masses, a tiny rake and a snuff spoon. In Wales, snuff was called "snisin."

**Tobacco boxes:** Tobacco boxes or presses were in evidence. From about 1565, when tobacco was introduced into Europe, containers were made to maintain tobacco properly. In the 17th century, the container had a hinged lid and was for carrying shredded tobacco (for use in cigarettes or pipes). In a taller variation, the box contained an inner lid which pressed down on the tobacco; hence the name tobacco press. It is traditionally thought that tobacco boxes were made with loose covers and snuff boxes were hinged. Tobacco for snuff was not cut into shreds, it was powdered. When cigarette smoking became common, shredded tobacco was used and people switched to tobacco jars, pouches and eventually to cigarette cases. Matches and their boxes replaced tinder boxes in about 1805. The early matches (vestas, lucifers, etc.) were formidable because of their tendency to self-ignite. They needed to be kept in metal containers. Sometimes the boxes used were snuff boxes modified by adding a striker.

**Vesta boxes:** Actual vesta boxes were manufactured in their own right, beginning in the 1850s. Vesta box was a term generally used for match boxes prior to the use of safety matches and was named after the Roman goddess of fire. The term was used until World War I, at which time the vesta was replaced by the safety match and the lighter. Depending on inclination, the vesta box was worn

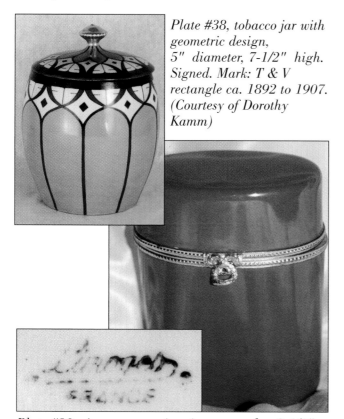

*Plate #38, tobacco jar with geometric design, 5" diameter, 7-1/2" high. Signed. Mark: T & V rectangle ca. 1892 to 1907. (Courtesy of Dorothy Kamm)*

*Plate #30, cigarette container in a rust color. 3-1/8" long, 2" wide, 4-1/4" high. Mark: Limoges France (Limoges Castel) date unknown.*

on a watch chain or in the pocket. It came in many shapes, some as fanciful as birds and shoes.

Boxes, be they beautiful or utilitarian add to the joy of our lives.

## Box Motifs

The subjects or motifs depicted on snuff boxes and the other precious objects deluxe, mirrored the prevailing moods and values of society and give us the opportunity to step back in time and view a physical manifestation of the styles of the time. Even though snuff boxes were small, they were not insignificant. They were considered indicative of social status and were lavished with attention to detail, design and decoration. The snuff box (*tabatiere*), patch box, *etui* or other small personal items were in effect a statement about the owner. Finely executed boxes were truly small works of art.

Ornate boxes became *de rigueur* for occasions of importance or to make a social statement. One example of the significance of snuff boxes was shown when portraiture was done of the wealthy and they included a snuff box in the setting. Many different styles of boxes existed since people of fashion wanted to be in the forefront of what was popular, wanted to show their wealth and panache and wanted to indulge in the fantastic if they could afford it. Fashionable people then as now wanted to coordinate what they were wearing. Since the snuff box was an accessory, albeit for the aristocracy an expensive one, they were chosen to match one's outfit. Like jewelry, decorative boxes were an expression of the individual's inclinations and the choice of the box emphasized the statement. Theme, color or activity were expressed through one's choice. Even the seasons were a factor, with lighter colors being used in spring and summer than in fall and winter.

Box motifs included a number of trends. One was the painting of the box in the style of favored artists of the day. You'll find the likes of a Boucher, Fragonard, Watteau, Lancret or a Nattier. Included in the works of some of these artists were cherubs, an incredibly popular motif.

Quite frequently, boxes were done in floral motifs or with floral designs complementing other scenes. Landscapes, river and sea scenes drew the attention and desires of the collector. Exterior and/or interior views of grand chateaux were frequently portrayed. *Fetes champetres*, rural escapades of the aristocracy, were a favored subject. Sporting, hunting and gaming scenes depicting the leisure activities beloved by the royals, were popu-

lar subjects for boxes. Portraits of royals, sweethearts or family members were also the vogue. Sometimes the portrait was painted on the inside of the lid, only to be seen when the box was open. Portraits were sometimes done in bas relief. Portrait boxes were often given before a trip as a reminder of a loved one. They could have secret compartments where love notes, messages or mementos could be placed.

Another motif depicted events of note. For example, numerous naval, military or historical exploits were commemorated. Coats-of-arms and dedications were also featured. Portraits of Napoleon Bonaparte were done in abundance, since Napoleon wanted to advance his importance and was very involved in supporting the French decorative arts.

Also used were Baroque, Rococo and Neo-Classical decorative motifs where arabesques, garlands, swags, medallions, cartouches, trophies, wreaths, trellis work, anthemions, scallops and baskets of fruit were featured on the top of many a box.

Themes of interest in society were shown such as the *Commedia dell' arte*, with scenes including Harlequin or other characters. Whimsy was shown on occasion with animals depicted wearing clothes or children humorously dressed as adults. Scenes depicting mythological subjects were used; after the Revolution, these themes took on greater importance and were used as analogies for the virtues that should be in existence. Oriental motifs understandably were ubiquitous given that China was the progenitor of porcelain. Some examples of this trend were *Chinoiserie* themes; the bursting pomegranate motif; and the use of the color celadon.

On occasion we find *trompe l' oeil*, mimicking semi-precious stones such as lapis lazuli, agate or malachite. These keepsakes could also be decorated in imitation of other precious items or in the shape of other things, such as a letter, a barrel or a fruit. Some boxes showed items in low relief such as animals. Other boxes were done in high relief in the form of people, flowers and fruit. A range of animals was characterized in high relief such as a dog, horse, goat, squirrel, reindeer, dolphin or lobster. (The book, *Animaux Boites Porcelaine* has wonderful examples.)

These artists and styles represent different aspects of society's tastes and changing moral attitudes. Often, after a popular artist had painted a piece, it was the custom that an engraver reproduced the piece on a small scale. This smaller copy would serve as the source for the design being transferred to porcelain in the form of a drawing. Engraving inventories were kept for this purpose by the factories. The engravings often served as a creative stimulus for a drawing, the porcelain artist possibly borrowed parts or perhaps the entire engraving might be copied. Some artists specifically included snuff box designs. There was an extensive inventory at the Royal Manufactory in Germany in 1770 which showed more than 1,000 engravings with such varied motifs as landscapes, figure pieces and flower pieces, leading one to the understanding that adapted works were used in abundance.

Boxes were made from a variety of materials. In addition to painted porcelains there were English enamels, Wedgwood jasperware, treen, tortoise shell, vernis Martin, mother of pearl, Japanese lacquer and other materials, plus sumptuous boxes made of gold and fine jewels and sometimes mounted with items from the Renaissance, ancient Roman or Grecian times.

These boxes, of porcelain or other materials, were often given the broad heading of snuff boxes, but they had many uses. Sometimes these elaborate boxes were given to honor an individual for a particular achievement. They might be given to show gratitude for heroic or exemplary behavior and some boxes were embellished with personal monograms. Kings and emperors used gold boxes as a form of payment for services provided. In some instances these boxes were then returned for money and could be given again to a new recipient. These so-called snuff boxes sometimes had the portrait of the giver and would be referred to as *boite a portrait*. These portraits could be painted on porcelain, ivory or other substances and mounted on the box.

In some cases gifts were enclosed in snuff boxes made of precious stones and metals. In other words, a gift in a gift. So snuff boxes proved to be the bearers of many delightful things. The revival in current production allows us to continue to be transported back to the grandeur of the past.

## Five Expressions of Porcelain

Although porcelain was produced in China by the Tang Dynasty (618-907), it was essentially unknown to Europeans until the early 18th century. The secret for its production was closely guarded and porcelain was regarded with awe and admiration. The European's regard for it, with its attributes of strength of substance, aspect of elusiveness and mystery of production, became an obsession.

Europeans wanted to make their own "china." Many set out to discover the knowledge possessed by the arcanists, those who knew the secret. After much time, trial and error and intrigue (which in one instance, lead to a situation that amounted to paid imprisonment) the secret was found out. The aristocracy demanded porcelain in huge quantities and many styles.

The royals found porcelain had a special aura. It was fragile and luminous and visually appealing. There was secrecy surrounding it, an all pervasive interest in obtaining it and a cachet to owning it; all of which gave impetus to the aristocracy of Europe to collect it with a passion. At one time, it was thought that porcelain had magical qualities such as warding off illness or serving as an indicator of poison.

Porcelain was more than a wonderful new substance, it became the defining innovative vehicle for art expression of the 18th century aristocracy. It was put to every conceivable use. In its many forms, porcelain conveyed numerous aspects of life. Whether the subject was personal, such as a family grouping or cultural as the *Commedia dell' arte*, the art of porcelain shone.

Five, three-dimensional art forms were developed:

1. One expression or form of the art of porcelain for the European Court is the miniature *tableaux*. The Court, which was the *sine qua non* of splendor, was the seat of luxury and excess. Fancy dress balls, masquerades, and garden parties were enjoyed. The Court was also taken by the exotic. These themes plus other conventional activities and inclinations were expressed in terms of porcelain in the production of miniature scenes for banquet tables. These *tableaux* or scenes could be very elaborate and emanate from the central theme of the event, with the idea possibly extending throughout to include tableware and clothing or costumes worn. An example being a wedding with a centerpiece depicting a temple of love surrounded by a scene evoking the prospect of a happy future.

2. Another aspect is elaborate decorative pieces made to satisfy the royal cravings: massive vases, some being over six feet tall; fantastic reticulated objects; various containers encrusted with flowers; clocks with exotic animals cavorting about. Anything that they could imagine and which was physically possible in the medium was made. To gild the lily, sometimes these fantastic objects were mounted in ormolu. Another manifestation of using

porcelain for decoration was the use of porcelain plaques. These could be incorporated into furniture, mirrors or other items.

3. The third expression is porcelain figures. They were three-dimensional depictions of individuals and couples who ranged from sturdy commoners to effete ladies and gentlemen. These figures varied in poses and affects. The figural pieces run from relatively unadorned to an involved scene on a pedestal surrounded by foliage. They show the playfulness of couples, the humor of farcial characters or the symbolism of different themes, such as love represented by birds and an open birdcage. Cultural pieces depicting the arts were also in evidence. Also portrayed were animals, mythology and various other themes.

4. The next category is the magnificent dinner services, tea and dessert sets which were made. The exquisite porcelain tableware services for the French court, Count Bruhl's Swan Service and Catherine the Great's banquet service, were incredible feats of porcelain artistry. In addition to the extravagant dinner sets, elaborate sets were made for serving tea, coffee, chocolate and desserts.

5. Finally, we have the porcelain personal accessories for men and women or to use the 18th century terms "gallantries" or "toys," which included snuff boxes and other decorative boxes. Items specifically for men included pipe bowls, swords with porcelain hilts and jacket buttons. Porcelain items made for women included earrings, thimbles, needle cases and vanity sets. Porcelain objects were also made for the writing or dressing table.

Porcelain was the current rage and obsession. Items produced in porcelain in its many forms covered the spectrum from the mundane to the magnificent. The royals were obsessed with the idea of possessing it and put their efforts into producing the finest objects possible. Porcelain was the pinnacle.

## A Look Back

One can acquire wonderful Limoges boxes when a collection of a friend or relative is handed down. By maintaining this collection, you preserve family history and treasures.

Another method of obtaining Limoges boxes is to blaze the trail of the collector. Given this inclination, your adventure will begin. Once you start this journey, you will find the joy of the chase and the thrill of discovery. You can find wonderful things at diverse places: estate sales, local antique shops and antique shows. If you are in the process of forming a collection you might want to consider a few things.

*Theme*: Do you want to go with a particular theme such as fruits and vegetables, flowers or classic boxes? Or do you want your collection to commemorate the special occasions in your life?

*Continuity and Change*: How does a new piece fit into your collection? Do you want to expand into different areas? How you define a collection changes over time.

*Provenance or Condition*: Is it unique or undamaged? Is this important to you? More on these subjects in Chapter 6, "Collecting Suggestions."

There is an ebb and flow to collecting as there is to any other joy in life. Have a grand time collecting!

*Plate #1, covered candy box with violet design, 5" diameter, 2-1/2" high. Mark: D & Co (Delignieres) ca. 1880-1900.*

Plate #3, collar button or stud box with pink roses and gilded collar, button and knob, 2-1/2" diameter, 1" high. Signed. Mark: ADK (A.Klingenberg), ca. 1890-1910.

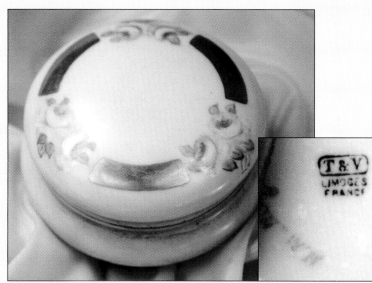

Plate #4, powder box with pink roses and bands of gold, 3-3/4" diameter, 2-3/8" high. Signed. Mark: T & V (Tressemanes [or Tressemann] & Vogt) ca. 1890-1910.

Plate #5, powder box with large pink roses and leaves, 3-3/4" diameter, 2-1/4" high. Mark: Elite (Bawo & Dotter) ca. 1900-1920.

Plate #7, button box with pink blossoms, 2-3/4" square, 2-1/8" high. Mark: B & Co (Bernardaud & Co.) Ca. 1900-1915.

Plate #8, powder box with violets, 4" diameter, 2-1/4" high. Mark: PL (La Porcelaine Limousine) ca. 1910-late 1930s.

Plate #9, accessory box, pate sur pate, with white cherubs on blue ground, 4-1/2" long, 4" wide, 2" high. Mark: C Tharaud (Camille Tharaud) ca.1920s.

Plate #10, hinged box with bird, 2-1/2" long, 2" wide, 1-1/4" high. Signed. Mark: Limoges France (Limoges Castel) date unknown.

Plate #11, hinged box with fleur de lys, 2-3/8" diameter, 1-1/8" high. Mark: Limoges France (Limoges France [unidentified company]) date unknown.

Plate #12, hinged box with floral central motif, 1-7/8" diameter, 1-1/4" high. Signed. Mark: Limoges France (Limoges France [unidentified company]) dated unknown.

Plate #13, hinged box with ellipsoid shape, central motif surrounded by gilding, 3" long, 1-3/4" wide, 1-1/4" high. Signed. Mark: Limoges France (Limoges Castel) date unknown.

Plate #14, hinged box with bee and olive wreath motif, 2-1/2" long, 2" wide, 1-1/4" high. Mark: Limoges France (Limoges Castel) date unknown.

Plate #17, hinged box bas relief of two fish (based on 16th century design), 3-1/4" long, 2-1/4" wide, 7/8" high. Mark: Chamart (Charles Martine) ca. 1960s.

Plate #19, conserve container with grape leaves and vines, 3-3/4" diameter, 5" high. Mark: T & V (Tressemanes & Vogt) ca. 1890-1907.

Plate #31, covered bonbon box with medallion design of cherubs and harp, 4-3/4" diameter. Dated: 1890. Signed. Backstamp is obliterated by a ground color. Design is based on Haviland plate (see article by Dorothy Kamm, HCIF). (Courtesy of Dorothy Kamm)

Plate #32, covered bonbon box with yellow roses, 8" diameter, 4-1/2" high. Signed. Mark: ADK ca. 1890s to 1910. (Courtesy of Dorothy Kamm)

Plate #33, covered bonbon box with art nouveau-style design, 4-3/4" diameter, 4-1/4" high. Signed. Mark: ADK ca. 1890s to 1910. (Courtesy of Dorothy Kamm)

Plate #34, puff box with yellow roses, 4-3/4" diameter. Mark: T & V rectangle ca. 1892 to 1917. (Courtesy of Dorothy Kamm)

*Plate #37, sardine box with painted sardine, 5-1/4" long, 4-3/16" wide, 1-5/8" high. Mark: T & V rectangle ca 1892 to 1907. (Courtesy of Dorothy Kamm)*

*Plate #39, dresser box with stylized roses, iridescent central area on top and interior of box, 2-1/2" square. Mark: PL (La Porcelaine Limousine) ca. 1910-1930. (Courtesy of Carole Willis)*

*Plate #40, powder box with roses, crosshatching and faux gem stones, 4-3/4" round. Signed. Mark: T & V (Tressemanes & Vogt) ca. 1890-1910. (Courtesy of Carole Willis)*

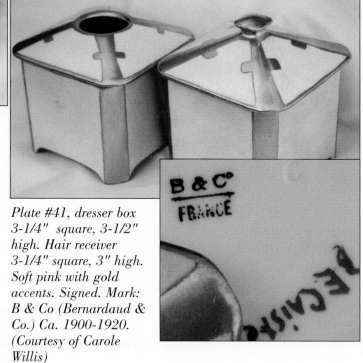

*Plate #41, dresser box 3-1/4" square, 3-1/2" high. Hair receiver 3-1/4" square, 3" high. Soft pink with gold accents. Signed. Mark: B & Co (Bernardaud & Co.) Ca. 1900-1920. (Courtesy of Carole Willis)*

*Plate #42, bonbonniere of orange crouched cat. 3" long, 2" wide, 2" high. Mark: Chamart (Charles Martine) ca.1960s. (Courtesy of Elayne Troute)*

Plate #43, bonbonniere curled cat on blue and white design. 3-1/4" long, 2" wide, 2" high. Mark: Limoges France, date unknown. Handpainted for Horchow collection. (Courtesy of Elayne Troute)

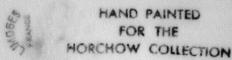

Plate #44, oval hinged box with picture of belled cat. 2-1/4" long, 1-1/2" wide, 1" high. Mark: Betty St. John (possible designer) and Rochard. Dated- mcmlxxiv. (Courtesy of Elayne Troute)

Plate #45, hinged box with cats in a basket. 2" long, 1-1/8" wide, 1-5/8" high. Mark: Chamart (Charles Martine) ca.1980s. (Courtesy of Elayne Troute)

Plate #46, hinged box with bowed front and decorated with embracing couple. Signed. 6-1/4" long, 3-3/4" high, 4" deep marked GDM. (Courtesy of Debby DuBay).

# CHAPTER 5

# Old and New Tales

## Fit For A King

The 18th century until the French Revolution was a time of decadence and elegant superficiality. Collection became a mania and self-indulgence a cornerstone of aristocratic life. Porcelain with all its appealing characteristics cast a spell of desire over Europe. Since Chinese porcelain preceded porcelain in Europe, Europeans collected Chinese Export pieces in prodigious quantity. Nobility in Europe even had rooms in their homes devoted to porcelain and porcelain collections. During Louis XIV's waning years and continuing through the Regency of the Duke of Orleans (before Louis XV was old enough to become King) a porcelain room was considered *de rigueur* in an aristocrat's home. Taken to the greatest excess, entire walls were completely covered with porcelain.

When the Europeans discovered the secret of porcelain production, porcelain factories became another way for royalty to display their status. They were considered to be second only to owning a palace. Porcelain as a luxury material was produced by and for the wealthy and essentially without consideration for price.

Royalty and aristocracy purchased porcelain factories, vying with one another in their attempts to produce items of note and advances in techniques. King Louis XV was involved with the production at Sevres and was known to sell the porcelain himself. Given the moneys available to them, royalty could satisfy its taste to its most ornate degree. Artists from many fields were commissioned to work on these creations. Porcelain production was the new and exciting creative outlet. It served as the vital new mode for expressing fashion, taste and art. It was the defining influence in the decorative arts.

But even the rarefied world of the French Court sometimes experienced unexpected changes. This time the ramifications effected the porcelain industry. What follows outlines what occurred in the evolution of porcelain use.

In 1709, as in earlier times, the French aristocracy was called upon to turn in its silver to help fill the coffers of the King. Fifty years later, both the French aristocracy and the middle class were asked to turn in its silver. For six months, King Louis XV had silver melted down non-stop to meet his expenses. This turn of events partially accounts for the lack of silver artifacts from the era. Due to the lack of silver, the wealthy shifted to ceramics. Fine porcelain at that time was viewed as an ethereal product. Serving pieces that had previously been made of gold and silver were now to be made in porcelain. Some say it was preferred over gold and silver. Certainly, it was sold in the finest stores, mounted in precious metals and kept in treasuries with gold, silver and jewels.

Since the aristocracy commissioned porcelain pieces to replace their silver items, be they large or small, this dramatically changed the porcelain industry. An amazing array of things was now to be made of porcelain, ranging from the prosaic to the elaborate, from bowls to chandeliers. Since porcelain was a poor conductor of heat, it proved to be an ideal holder for the fashionable beverages of society: coffee, tea and chocolate. Dinner services for the nobility were elaborate and contained many items we would not expect in our contemporary services: asparagus dishes, *ecuelles*, mustard pots, butter tubs, ice cream cups and wine glass coolers, to name a few. In addition to utilitarian items a category existed which was called "toys" which included sybaritic items such as perfume bottles and snuff boxes. The French influence was evidenced in the production of snuff boxes as it was with the other arts; its designs and concepts being the ideal to be emulated by the rest of Europe.

The French Court, from which the dominant

culture emanated, lived life in a grand manner. The aristocracy in Europe sought out all that was elegant, refined or unusual. The Court at Versailles, where luxury and decoration were more important than practicality, was the epitome of magnificence and splendor. It was the font of taste in art, architecture and language. By virtue of this, French was the language of many European courts. In Russia and Germany, French was the language of all educated people. (An extreme example of its undeniable pervasiveness occurred at the Battle of Boyne, in Ireland. The commands were issued in French!) Europe was infused with French influence. It is no wonder it was referred to as, "the French Europe."

Courtiers and ladies of the French Court were an extravagant and self-indulgent sort. They dined on the finest foods, drank the best wines and possessed incredible art, furniture and *objets de vertu* (including snuff boxes). Initially, snuff was thought to have both preventative and curative properties. Over time, the taking of snuff became a social activity. Europe followed France's lead in fashion and snuff box collecting was no exception.

Proper snuff taking became a high accomplishment for the European aristocracy, and developed into an indicator of refinement carried out in a specific structured way and it was spoken of as *l'art de priser* or *l'exercise de la tabatiere*. In addition to the proper usage, the box was very important because it was an indication of the owner's social status, prosperity and sense of aesthetics. Possession of a snuff box was essential to complete the gentleman's attire. The form, color and decoration of one's snuff box was quite significant. Individuals had their portraits painted depicting them holding their snuff box which represented the person's sophistication, fashion sense and importance.

Snuff taking and the need for elaborate boxes provided an outlet for individual creativity. It was a mode of obtaining variety in one's life. For the sake of variety, one could indulge in many snuff types, scents, containers and brands. People could show off their creative inclinations by their choice in their new and fashionable snuff box.

Snuff taking also served a social purpose. It could be used as a device in conversation, in relation to the issue of snuff taking, the style of a recent purchase or as a sign of the bond of friendship. Snuff taking also revealed characteristics, attitudes and manners. One group particularly served by snuff boxes and snuff taking was politicians since the use of the box afforded them time to stall when confronted with difficult or embarrassing questions.

At the peak of usage, snuff taking became a common experience. By the time the masses engaged in snuff taking, the less desirable habits of snuff taking were evident. An example is the habit of less than fastidious women eating and taking snuff at the same time. What occurred was an unappealing mixture ended up on their upper lip. As one can imagine it was not a pleasant sight. As is the case with any other fad, snuff taking fell out of fashion.

Before snuff fell out of fashion Madame de Pompadour, mistress to King Louis XV of France and a woman of many interests and accomplishments, was very involved in collecting and porcelain production. She and the King helped implement the beginning of Sevres, the Royal porcelain. Not limiting herself just to porcelain for the table, Madame de Pompadour is said to have had a snuff box for every day of the year, including many Sevres boxes. However, she brought the collecting of porcelain snuff boxes into vogue among the ladies of the Court. She took collecting to the point of absurdity. In one instance, she went so far as to have a winter garden, at her chateau at Bellevue, filled with scented, life-sized, natural appearing (soft paste) porcelain flowers including tulips, jonquils, lilies, anemones, carnations, hyacinths and roses. This excess caused quite a scandal.

For the future Louis XVI's marriage to Marie Antoinette in 1770, the Sevres factory wanted to make a gift. They decided a fitting "cadeau" would be a porcelain copy of the Royal Palace at Rheims as a centerpiece table decoration. They worked on this for many years. In her penchant for porcelain, she ordered a set of dinnerware, each plate of which took two months to complete. In addition to immersing herself in porcelain objects at Versailles, Marie Antoinette also delighted in them at Petit Trianon, indulging in the style of the Court in which playing at being a shepherd or shepherdess was the vogue. There she had constructed two dairies, a dwelling for herself, a farm, a cow shed, an aviary and a mill. The residents of her farm were picked to represent ideal peasants (as they were depicted in paintings at the time). The animals were also selected with care and were washed, perfumed and beribboned. She enjoyed playing at being the rustic and outfitted herself with milk jugs and churns made of fine porcelain to do the chores.

In addition to the French, many other Europeans were taken by the porcelain collecting craze and the taking of snuff. Augustus II, Elector of Saxony and King of Poland, was one of the driving forces in the discovery of porcelain in Europe (1709) and the founder of the Meissen factory. He was a man consumed by porcelain. He was dubbed the "King of China Maniacs." He spent enormous sums for individual pieces of porcelain that took his fancy.  At one point, he exchanged an entire regiment of soldiers with the King of Prussia for a set of 48 large vases! He referred to china as "the bleeding bowl of Saxony," since he spent so much on his collection. His passion led to the discovery of porcelain. It was said, that he cared more for his porcelain factory than for his children. Not content to just have a tremendous collection of porcelain and a porcelain factory, he dedicated a palace to housing it. He then displayed his collection there, which included just under 36,000 pieces.

Porcelain and snuff boxes overlap again in the personage of Count Heinrich von Bruhl (1700-1763), Prime Minister of Saxony and Director of the Meissen porcelain factory. Though not classified as jewelry, an appropriate snuff box was essential to the well-dressed man. Count Bruhl had an opulent and extensive wardrobe, with each outfit having a particular cane and snuff box to complete it. These ensembles were illustrated in a folio which the Count's valet presented to him for his judgment on his attire for the day. When the Count died, nearly 700 snuff boxes were put up for sale. During his directorship, Meissen produced large quantities of porcelain snuff boxes. Bruhl's indulgence even extended to tableware. He had a china service made, known as the "Swan" service, which included 2,000 pieces.

Charlotte, wife of England's King George III, was referred to as "Snuffy Charlotte," due to her excessive indulgence in snuff. She exemplified the expression, going from the ridiculous to the sublime. Charlotte had a pair of frogs which she had trained to make croaking noises when she tapped on her snuff box.  Now to the sublime, she had in her snuff box collection several wonderful snuff box-music box combinations.

Her son, King George IV, was also a profuse snuff-taker. His daily ritual required 12 varieties of snuff for his indulgence. Naturally, he was very involved in snuff box collecting to the point of obsession. He had hundreds of exquisite gold and gem studded snuff boxes for his personal use. At his coronation, snuff boxes were gifted to all the foreign representatives. He also gave them as gifts at the signing of any treaty (which brought complaints from Parliament concerning the amount spent per box). He had a special room at Windsor

Castle specifically for different varieties of snuff.

An interesting story regarding snuff boxes includes King George IV (Prince Regent at the time) and Beau Brummell, the legendary style setter. As the story goes, the King wanted and obtained one of Brummell's snuff boxes, which the King claimed could be exchange for the box of Brummell's choosing. When it came time to go through with the replacement, the King was no longer as positively inclined toward Brummell. (Because Brummell had slighted a clergyman in a social situation related to snuffing.) The King went back on his promise. Brummell, out of the King's favor and a debtor, left the country. Upon the disposition of Brummell's estate at auction a snuff box was sold and it is told that when inviting bids for the box, the lid was opened and a scrap of paper fell out with a note indicating Brummell's displeasure with the incident. It's amazing the power snuff boxes have over people.

William Pitt, Prime Minister of England was known to be a popular figure and when he resigned from office it was said that snuff boxes "rained" on him for a month.

Lord Petersham of England, later Earl of Harrington (1780-1851), was a snuff connoisseur. He, as did others of his inclination, had rooms dedicated to storing and preparing snuff. In his snuff room Lord Petersham had cabinets for day and evening snuff. He indulged himself with an enormous array of snuff boxes and he placed one interesting restriction on their use. A box once used could not be used again for the next twelve months. On one occasion, upon being complemented on a Sevres snuff box, he responded, "It's a nice summer box, but would not do for winter wear."

King Frederick the Great of Prussia (1712-1786) was enamored with snuff boxes. He commissioned exceedingly lavish snuff boxes, including porcelain ones, which were superlative. He is said to have considered the visual arts in a broad sense, with snuff boxes being subsumed under that heading. At the time of his death he had amassed for his own personal collection more than 1,500 boxes. Something that makes this even more amazing is that he seldom used a snuff box, preferring to keep snuff loose in his pockets. For his annual trip from Potsdam to Berlin for the winter holiday, he included in his entourage of companions, servants and belongings was a chest filled with the 100 snuff boxes specifically selected for use during the vacation.

According to Snowman, in *18th Century Gold Boxes of Europe*, Voltaire in visiting Potsdam in

1750 said, "I am in France here. Only my own tongue is spoken. German is reserved for addressing soldiers and horses." Again the supremacy of French culture is seen.

Porcelain products were also treasured in the Russian Court, which (although wealthy) was primitive. As an insight into this aspect we find, in 1634, Tsar Michael issued an edict that stated that snuff-takers who were caught using for the second time were to have their noses amputated. In the 18th century, it was still primitive but the Court was desirous of beautiful things.

Catherine the Great of Russia had a Sevres service made for her in 1779 which included more than 700 pieces, enough to serve a banquet for 60. She received her first snuff box, which was studded with diamonds, when she was 14, from Empress Elizabeth of Russia. Presently one can visit the Gold Room at the Hermitage and see a breathtaking array of gold boxes from years of royal collecting.

Interest in porcelain in its various forms and uses consumed Europe in the 18th century. Not only kings, but their subjects, were seized by this passion. Great families commissioned extensive services running into hundreds of pieces, decorated with crests, flowers, "jeweling" and gilding. Accompanying pieces, such as centerpieces, figurines and *tableaux* for the table or sideboard were made in porcelain for curiosity's and amusement's sake. Whether for diversion or practical use, if it was porcelain it took many guises and it was desired.

In an effort to broaden their experiences, wealthy Europeans went on the "grand tour," with a stay in Paris a must on their itinerary. They came home with suitcases packed with French porcelain. Porcelain figures and vases, beautiful in their own right, were often mounted in gold, silver or ormolu. Porcelain in its myriad forms had to be possessed.

France continued producing outstanding porcelain. Social change, which was evident in the changing styles of art and literature, as well as porcelain, were just the harbinger of things to come. The social unrest that accompanied the self-indulgence of the French royalty and precipitated the French Revolution brought about massive change. As a result, the French nobility disposed of many of their treasures, including their collections of snuff boxes, porcelains and other items of note. This however, augmented the collections of the English and others throughout Europe.

During the heyday of the 18th century, the most wonderful porcelain to ever exist was made. Today we are the recipients of these treasures from the past. Additionally, these creations have served to inspire the rededication to innovation and style in porcelain box making.

## Interview with Jan Cruikshank

Fine porcelain objects were once limited to kings and queens, but times have changed, and they are now available to us. The appeal of porcelain: the sheen, translucency, fine line and all the basic properties still continue. When looking at a finely painted Limoges box, we are getting to personally experience a miniature work of art. I asked Jan Cruikshank, owner of Coleman's Antiques, knowledgeable dealer, long-time seller of Limoges boxes, Limoges porcelain and other fine antiques, as well as proprietor of a Haviland matching service, to share with us some information on Limoges products.

*Q: When a collector enters your shop to find a Limoges box or other item, what would be your words of wisdom about collecting?*
A: Do your homework and know your marks. If in doubt, ask the dealer to put the information in writing and ask for a refund if it's incorrect.

*Q: Can you speak to the issue of quality and breakage in porcelain collection and Limoges boxes?*
A: Quality is in the making and the mark. Look for cracks, chips, poor painting, a damaged hinge or clasp.

*Q: Any suggestions on cleaning and protection?*
A: Porcelain can be washed in a mild soap with lukewarm water. In respect to the issue of protection, one can use Velcro dots, to act as buffers, by placing them strategically on the back of the piece.

*Q: What would you consider the most important thing or things about collecting Limoges boxes?*
A: Know your marks, study styles, etc. Do your homework.

*Q: Any ideas on telling an old box from a new one?*
A: Style, color and signs of wear. Don't rely upon marks entirely because of possible fakes. If the piece looks like it is brand new, it probably is.

# CHAPTER 6
## For the Collector

## Collecting Suggestions

*Current values or let the buyer beware*: Current value, worth, cost or price, in the context of antiques and collectibles, is open to interpretation and a number of considerations. Some of the concepts include: intricacies of design, materials and color, age, if the piece is signed, previous owner or provenance, repair, damage, uniqueness, marks (with all their inherent problems) and, when relevant, existing packaging.

If the dealer purchased the piece at a good price he/she may be willing to pass part of the savings along to you. Conversely, if top dollar was paid the price will remain high.

Dealer knowledge can also affect cost. I purchased a collectible piece from a dealer who didn't normally deal in Limoges boxes and who asked me to set the price! Try to enter the marketplace with as much knowledge as you can. The more you know the more likely you are to make an informed decision when purchasing collectibles.

The concept of retail price for antiques and secondary market collectibles is an issue with many levels. At a particular strata, such as in the finest auction houses and retail firms, there is a given range in which a piece will be known to sell. There might be fluctuations due to factors in the marketplace, but these pieces remain fairly stable.

Moving down from the *creme de la creme*, one sees many different levels of quality, provenance, repair, damage, rarity, until finally they are subject to fads, whims and fancies. When things are popular or fashionable the demand and prices go up. If a lot of people then realize they own that item and bring it into the marketplace in quantity, the market gets flooded, and prices go down.

Another issue that contributes to price is where you buy an item. If you find an item at a garage sale, and you know its worth, and the price is low, you're lucky. We all hope for the great find. Going up the ladder are estate sales, legitimate general auction houses, local antique stores and shows, each level escalating in price. Purchasing on the Internet has added a whole spectrum of changes.

Workmanship and condition are two other variables in the price of an object. The more intricate the detailing or crafting of an item, the greater the likelihood of a higher price. Also, if the item is in pristine condition and sometimes in the original packaging, the price will be higher. Due to changing variables, prices change.

An excellent point was brought to my attention by a knowledgeable collector and friend: Buying and selling in a particular field, you learn the current value of items in that field. You have to gain as much knowledge as possible about your field of collecting, since you cannot depend on the general level of knowledge of dealers.

The uniqueness of a piece is a further consideration, thus the rarity of a piece is a factor, whether it is old or not. If the piece is a significant remaining example of a particular craftsperson or factory it would be considered rare or unique and, therefore, more costly.

The material that the item is made from, the prowess of the maker, the intricacy of the work, the history of the piece and current trends will all affect the price.

*Damage*: Look for damage! Use your sense of touch in addition to sight. A low priced item can mean a flawed piece. The dealer, upon purchasing, may not have noticed any damage or may have damaged the piece in transit and is trying to get rid of it. Price tags may cover damage, check underneath them. If the bottom of the piece is obscured by a felt covering, ascertain if it covers damage.

The issue of flaws in items is not as simple as one might initially think. Under certain circumstances, if an item is flawed in firing, the value or price is not diminished. However, a crackle or crazing, a network of thin cracks in the glaze, would normally be considered a flaw. Also, when a piece is repaired, it affects the price, so remember to look for repairs.

*Negotiations*: If you want to negotiate a better price for a piece, ascertain whether the dealer negotiates. The phrase "What is your best price?" gets to the point without denigrating the merchandise. I've spoken to dealers about this issue, and talking about how bad or damaged a piece is in an attempt to try to reduce its price can be construed as offensive. After all, some say, if you feel the piece is so inferior why buy it? If you decide to ask for a discount, be discreet; don't ask in front of other customers. The dealer may be selling something for full price to someone and may out of circumstance need to say no, even though if asked discreetly he may have said yes.

*Detail*: In Limoges porcelain or boxes, as with anything else, there are degrees of excellence. When you are deciding on a piece look at the detail work. Transfer (or decal) pieces are considered of lesser quality than hand-painted pieces, but even within this category there are distinctions. (See section on surface decoration.)

Of higher quality than transfers is amateur porcelain painting done either at home or in a class setting. Around the turn of the last century this was a hobby that both men and women enjoyed. Currently, porcelain painting is having a resurgence and classes are readily available. The end-product of amateur painting, as one might expect, is quite variable. I have seen lovely decorative pieces with hand painting where the work is quite good and found some work to be abysmal. You have to judge each piece on its own merits.

The highest quality is professional decoration done at a factory or decorating studio. Even at this level there is variation. Some pieces have character and interest, but lack detail. True excellence, the *chef d'oeuvre*, is the piece that has it all: design, harmony, workmanship, detail, color, and balance.

*Consistency*: A fine piece should be consistent in quality. For example, when looking at the hinges on a fine porcelain snuff box, the craftsmanship should be consonant with the rest of the piece.

*Seconds*: Historically, pieces that were not first quality were sometimes sold. They may have had a slash through the mark to indicate it was a second. The sale of undecorated white rejects in 1793, 1800, 1804, 1813 and 1848 by the Sevres factory introduced questionable merchandise into the marketplace. These pieces were then enhanced with costly forms of decoration and more-or-less appropriate marks. These wares have muddied the waters of legitimate Sevres. As one could imagine, they sold quite well.

*The Hunt*: Depending on the individual, a good portion of the enjoyment of collecting is the activity that leads up to the purchase. Collecting knowledge, sharing with friends and collectors, defining interests, planning your field or specialty, and perusing museums, historical homes, auction houses and other venues can be great fun.

*Comparison shopping*: A resource for comparing a known, pictured or displayed antique piece with a comparable antique piece in the marketplace or private collection is available at Yale University at the Mabel Brady Garvan Collection. You can also check your local museum or university art collection.

*Final note: Love the piece!* Does it speak to you? Does it tug at your heart? Does it say, "buy me and take me home?" You'll know when the time comes! ENJOY!

## Surface Decoration

In differentiating a hand-painted box from a transfer, there are four common variations in boxes with transfers:

1. A box may have a transfer used instead of painting.

2. A box that may have a transfer as well as highlighting stroke-work enhancing the design.

3. Boxes can have both a transfer (usually the center design) and some hand-painting.

4. A fourth variation is boxes with some background color put in with a transfer.

In boxes that have this "painting," one might see a designation on the bottom of the box that says, "Hand-painted." Sometimes the artist who did the minor stroke-work or background color on a transfer piece would then sign the piece, possibly prominently. In recent times, some manufacturers indicate "REHAUSSE MAIN" on the bottom of the piece which means "enhanced."

*1. In this piece you can see disjointedness of design. The sprigs of flowers do not flow, like a hand-painted piece.*

*3. This porcelain paperweight has a transfer surrounded by hand-painted accenting stroke work.*

*2. This particular box shows many things:*
*A) Enhanced stroke work in white can be seen on the two central flowers and the wings and tail of the bird.*
*B) Tearing of the transfer or decal shows on the left side of the design directly above the branch; there is a break in the stem of the leaf and a piece missing from a leaf.*
*C) Tearing of the edge of a design, on the left side the large leaf has spiked edges except for a straight edge where the transfer tore.*

*4.*
*The lamp base is an example of hand-paint-ed background, the sky, with a transfer in the foreground.*

## Hand Painted or Transfer

*Exterior*: The following directions are given as if you are holding a box in your hand and are looking at it. In looking at the center design, one can tell the difference between a hand-painted design and a transfer by turning the top of the box at an angle. If the design is flat and you can see dots making up the picture, this is the sign of a transfer. You could use a magnifying glass and if you see the dot pattern this indicates a transfer. Another aspect of transfers that you might see on old boxes is that a transfer can sometimes tear. If the design ends abruptly in a straight or ragged edge, that indicates a transfer. Even without a tear, upon close inspection you can see where the transfer ends. If the bottom outside portion of the box has transfers as decoration, it stands to reason that the box is decorated by transfer, since a hand-painted box would most likely be painted on the bottom portion also.

*Interior*: Hand-painted boxes usually have a hand-painted design on the enclosed part of the box, either the top or base of the bottom portion. So there are usually no hand-painted interior designs on transfer pieces.

*Back*: If the box decoration is not done with a transfer, but is hand-painted, it could be marked "PEINT MAIN," French for "painted by hand," written either in cursive or by machine printing. The signature, initials or number of the artist will sometimes be placed on the bottom of the box. The initials of the artist can be worked into the design on the face of the box. (See also the manufacturer's mark section and the chapter on fakes.)

## Fakes, Fudging, and Fundamental Differences

An infamous name in reproductions and copyists of covered boxes, porcelain and Limoges enamels is Samson. In the 19th century, the French firm of Edme Samson et Cie, of Paris, imitated various makers of fine china, enamel work and enameled boxes with incredible precision. The firm, the House of Samson, began in 1845. Edme Samson was a china decorator. As the story goes, his son, Emile, began the "reproduction business." It started with an incident which involved the Grand Duke of Russia. He wanted copies of Limoges porcelain and Samson complied.

People continued to use the firm, for differing reasons. Some just wanted to replace their broken dinner ware. The business later extended to making copies of items of interest to collectors. These copies, supposedly, were initially made and marked with the Samson mark. Over time, some of these marks have been altered in some fashion. The firm advertised that it made: "Reproductions of Ancient Works emanating from the Museums and from private collections." The business was passed on to successive sons; passing out of family hands in the mid-1960s.

During the 1860s Sampson Bridgwood, a potter from Staffordshire, England made wares evocative of Limoges' and used similar ground colors and gilding. The mark he used was, "LIMOGES PORCELAINE OPAQUE," which was impressed into the piece in a circle. It would come as no surprise that the stamp resembled a legitimate Limoges mark.

Fakes, frauds and imitators are a continual problem. As stated by Ruth Webb Lee, in *Antiques, Fakes and Reproductions* in 1938, "the earlier the copy the better the quality is apt to be, for being sold contemporaneously with the originals, they had to be very well done."

When looking for an antique or collectible piece keep in mind that even if these items were sold as reproductions or re-issues when they were new, time has passed and it is difficult for us to tell the difference between an authentic piece and a copy of a later date. Pearsall, in the *Illustrated Guide to Collecting Antiques*, related a story of a dealer, prior to World War I, who went to Meissen and ordered figures from a pattern book for about $100. The dealer then altered them to make them appear old and subsequently sold them in England for over $3,000. Buyers were fooled then. Now the distinction would be even more difficult to make.

Further complicating the fakery issue is that the Europeans were enamored with Chinese motifs. The Europeans worked in a Chinese manner, even going so far as making marks imitative of Chinese marks. Concurrently, Chinese items, which were being imported for the European trade, sometimes imitated European themes. It is not surprising that there is confusion.

Commissioned copies are another source of fake pieces in the marketplace. Even though they were known as copies when initially commissioned, it becomes increasingly difficult to perceive that fact as time elapses. As stated by Mills in *How to Detect Fake Antiques*, "They pass from collection to collection, come on the market, linger on gallery walls, and somewhere along the line their provenance becomes embroidered."

In looking at boxes, keep a watch for so called enhancing physical changes in your prospective purchase. Beware if the bottom of the box has an area that has been scraped off or painted over, for this could indicate that a prior owner did not want the manufacturer known and obliterated the mark. Another problem occurs when unscrupulous peo-

*FAKE! Not a Limoges mark.*

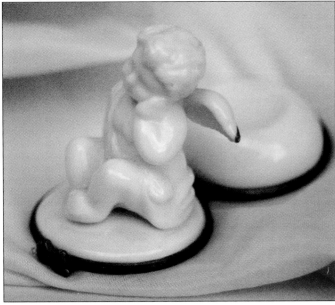

*Note: Hinge opens much wider than a legitimate Limoges hinge. FAKE!*

ple falsely age a piece.

In your pursuit of boxes or porcelain, you might attend an auction. Be aware of a tactic used by some auctioneers. When selling items, they intersperse reproductions or less desirable items of questionable value to broaden their selling base and increase the number of items to be sold. I attended an auction where an auctioneer was selling what appeared to be a new openwork ceramic bowl from Europe. He alluded to how items like this (implying antiques) are worth a lot. But the piece being auctioned was neither old, nor porcelain, nor worth a lot. Don't get caught up in the moment Land buy carelessly.

Be aware, too, of the differences in hand-painted items. White blanks were shipped into the United States to satisfy the needs of people doing decorative painting as a hobby or professionally, around the turn of the century. Therefore, you will notice different degrees of proficiency in painting on porcelains. These pieces could even be signed or initialed by the "artist." Even though a piece says "Limoges," it does not mean it is professionally painted.

The practice of importing blank porcelain continues. In shopping for supplies for a china painting class I attended, I came across blanks for covered boxes, supplied either with or without hinged covers. Be aware that the antique you are looking at may be a contemporary piece.

Mary Frank Gaston in *The Collector's Encyclopedia of Limoges Porcelain* (1996), mentions that a few years after her first edition, "modern pieces made in Taiwan began to appear at flea markets and were offered by wholesale houses specializing in reproductions. Such pieces were marked with a *fleur-de-lys* and a banner underneath containing the words 'Limoges China.'"

In early 1999, I attended a major gift show and saw that small hinged boxes are now being produced which have the *fleur-de-lys* and banner with the words LIMOGES CHINA marked on the underside.

Another issue in relation to reproductions comes to the fore at some antique shows and shops. Dealers will carry both old, new and imitative boxes. It is up to the collector to be knowledgeable since the dealer or representative may not know the age of a piece or whether it is legitimate.

I recently attended a major gift show and saw a ceramic box with the initials of a prestigious company from Germany painted on the back of the box and a paper sticker attached which indicated the box was made in China. When discussing this issue early in 1998, with Mark Chervenka, the editor of *Antique & Collectors Reproduction News*, I came to understand that there is a legal loop hole employed by foreign manufacturers. Marks on the bottom of a piece are considered decorations. Foreign manufacturers import porcelain products into the United States and use a removable paper sticker which must list "Made in ..." followed by the country of origin, as the indicator of the source. In conjunction with the paper sticker, they then print what we might consider back marks on the piece; therefore, when someone removes the paper sticker we don't know the country of origin. Reproductions continue to be a problem! Deal with reputable sources!

In direct relationship to this, I was in a local shop in August 1998 and saw the products of a manufacturer who is producing imitations of Limoges boxes. These did not have a manufacturer's mark. They will be confusing on the secondary market.

In porcelain, sometimes it is difficult to differentiate makers or factories. Especially in old porcelain, production people who engaged in design and art work did not have stable work situations; they often moved due to religious or monetary necessity. When they moved to a new location, their work influenced their co-workers. This blending of design ideas was also affected by the availability of books with samples of decorative ornamentation. A particular motif, therefore, would not definitely indicate a particular designer, factory or country of origin. In addition to the difficulty of differentiating the design source, marks were an issue, since most antique boxes were not marked. Unfortunately, problems with dating and ascribing origins of boxes are often insoluble. The issue of copying continues to be problematic.

Manufacturer's marks are also subject to fakery and fudging. Their authenticity is often in question. Factories frequently imitated other factory styles and marks. I recently (1998) came across a fake Limoges mark on an older box. When I turned the box over to see the manufacturer's mark, I saw a creative attempt to lead one to think the box was legitimate. The mark was "Amoges," with the first letter looking like a capital "L" and a slash coming down, like the descending line on an "A."

Marks were copied, approximated, modified, scraped and written over. Finally, I will repeat the common knowledge on this problem: the mark can be a supporting piece of evidence on an item that appears to be authentic, but it should not be the defining factor.

Collectors cannot become knowledgeable solely from reading and looking at photographs. Prior to considering purchasing, try to handle representative pieces to gain knowledge of the feel and distinctions of the real item. Study the qualities that are characteristic of a fine piece so you can recognize these qualities when you are ready to buy. Museums, museum libraries, antique shops, shows, auctions and auction catalogs are venues which will help you in your efforts to learn.

Time, experience, and knowledge will be your final teachers. When buying on the secondary market, purchase from knowledgeable and reputable dealers.

# Glossary

Anthemion: Classical motif. Suggesting spreading leaves or petals. Also known as the honeysuckle motif.

Arabesques: Scrolling, undulating and intertwining plant forms, sometimes interspersed with fruits and flowers. This motif was used in the Renaissance and in later European art.

Arcanists: Workmen claiming to know the secret of porcelain production. This area was rife with problems, as some arcanists possessed knowledge of porcelain techniques and chemical make-up and others were frauds.

Arcanum: Latin for "secret." When people were searching for the key to porcelain production, the world was still mired in superstition. People believed that gold and silver could be made artificially if the right combination of ingredients were mixed. Some felt the lacking ingredient was a liquid referred to as "arcanum." In addition to being considered the entree to the production of gold, it was thought to be the panacea for all illness.

Art Nouveau: Style of art in France whose peak was 1890-1905. The name came from the art dealer, Siegfried (or Samuel) Bing whose gallery, La Maison de l'Art Nouveau, was carrying the works. Art Nouveau is characterized by naturalism, simplicity and quality of craftsmanship.

Atelier: French for workshop or studio, usually used in connection with artists, artisans and aligned workers.

Bacchus: Latin equivalent of Dionysis, the Greek god of fertility and wine.

Back stamp or back mark: Also known as mark. Mark or symbol on the back of a piece which indicates the location and period of manufacture. Other marks on the back might include the artist's name or abbreviation and the gilder's symbol. (See sections on fakes and manufacturer's marks.)

Barbotine: French word for slip or decoration done with slip; also, term used for French faience in 19th century.

Baroque: From the Portuguese word barroco (or Italian, barocco), meaning irregular shaped pearl. Dramatic and sensual art style dating from about 1600s-1760, including Rococo. French proponents include: Boucher, Fragonard and Watteau. Decorating motifs from this style could include cartouches, C-scrolls, S-scrolls, foliated scrolls, grotesques, whorls or volutes (like the top of an Ionic capital), also known in France as Louis XIV style.

Bas-relief: French for low relief. Slightly raised designs are indicative of this technique.

Bat: The gelatin or glue pad used instead of tissue paper in one type of transfer printing.

Bijouterie: Jewelry or objets d'art. Also, the display case for displaying these small objects.

Biscuit or bisque: Pottery or porcelain fired once and not glazed.

Bodkin: Special large-eyed needle for threading ribbons, etc., through clothing. Bodkins were carried, rather than stored, so mending could take place at the time of need, and also because needles and pins were expensive and kept close at hand. Bodkins were carried in cases, wallets, etc.

Body: Main section of a piece, rather than handles, etc.; also, raw materials used in making clay products (in hard paste porcelain, the term paste is used).

Boite: French for box.

Boite a Cathedrale: Box with motif featuring Cathedral architecture.

Bombe: Bulbous or bulging.

Bone china: Hard paste porcelain with calcined bone, initially produced by Josiah Spode in 1794.

Bone porcelain: Soft paste porcelain with bone ash, made initially about 1750.

Bougie box: 18th century box containing coiled candle taper.

Bric a brac: Thought to come from the French phrase de bric et de broc—meaning by hook or by crook, (in other words, odds and ends). These included porcelain, glass and silver with artistic merit.

Cailloute: Pebble-shaped design or assorted circles, also called crazy-paving. A design used to break up broad areas of color, to make the piece more visually appealing.

Camaieu: French term for a painting technique where several shades of a color and only that color, are used on one piece. Monochromatic use of a color.

Cartouche: Stylized shield or oval shape used as a visual framing device that could be surrounded with scroll work or gilding. Also, decoration in the form of an unrolling scroll.

Celadon: Typically known as a light gray-green glaze, although celadon can range from putty colored through different greens to sea green. Spotted celadon ware can have spots of reddish brown. The color was thought to show change in contact with poison. French term started in the 17th century thought to derive from the color of the coat worn by the hero who played the part of Celadon in a production called L' Astree, by Honore d' Urfe. Another explanation for the name is related to the Sultan of Egypt, Salah-ed-din, although this is disputed. The ware was thought by some to resemble jade. From the 18th century forward the glaze was used on porcelain, in addition to stoneware.

Ceramic or keramic: From the Greek word keramos, meaning clay. The term was used for all items made from that material.

Chambrelan: French for home hand painter (independent decorator).

Champleve: Type of enameling in which the metal base is grooved out to form a pattern and the grooves are then filled with colored enamel.

Chatelaine: French for mistress of the chateau. Triangular clasp or hook attached to a decorative metal plate or waist chain from which keys, etuis, pomaders (or vinaigrettes), scent bottles, snuff boxes, watches, needle (or bodkin) cases or other needed items were hung. The number and type of items used was based on personal taste, but on the average five items were worn. Used in the 17th century, the chatelaine became more decorative and elaborate in the 18th century. At that time, it was a popular bride's gift. For formal occasions it could be embellished with enamels and gems. Men also used chatelaines. At the end of the 19th century they fell out of use.

Chef d'oeuvre: French for masterpiece.

China: Originally referred to wares exported from China in the 18th century. The term is now commonly used in reference to porcelain and pottery tablewares.

Chinoiserie: Chinese motif used by European artists depicting Western concepts of Eastern themes. This was one expression of the 18th century obsession with things exotic.

Cie or compagnie: French for company. Box back notation.

Commedia dell' arte or Italian comedy: Impromptu plays, performed starting in the 16th century, with plots revolving around situations involving love and containing mistaken identities, intrigue and satire. Some of its stock characters were portrayed in porcelain, such as Harlequin.

Commode: French term for low set of drawers, sometimes represented in porcelain boxes.

Comport: Footed dessert bowl or plate, which was called a compote around the 1920s. An aligned piece was the compotier, a dish or bowl for serving compote (cooked, whole fruit). The compotier may or may not have been footed.

Comte: French term for count.

Courtiers: Attendants at court.

Cowrie or Cowry shell: Warm water mollusk whose shell was thought to prevent evil, increase fertility and ensure a long life. Used for the body of snuff boxes. (genus Cypraea)

Crackle: (French, *craquelure*). Crazing done intentionally.

Crazing: A network of thin cracks in the glaze.

Creamware: English glazed earthenware, also known as *faience fine*.

Curio: Abbreviation of the word curiosity. In the 18th century and before when possible, people of wealth collected valuable rarities and curiosities from distant and exotic locales. These were displayed in cabinets which came to be called curio cabinets. An aligned word is bric a brac.

*Curiosa:* Natural curiosities such as unusual shells, stones or wood which were collected for display or were mounted in snuff boxes.

Decal: Term in common use in the United States for a transfer. This refers to a lithographic process by which designs or patterns are transferred to a piece of paper; which can be cut (as desired) and adhered to a surface.

*Decor:* French for decoration. Box back notation.

*Depose:* French for patented. Box back notation.

Diaper: Diamond, trellis or rectangular shaped border pattern, used to reduce the vividness of the ground colors in porcelain.

Dresden china: Designation in England for Meissen porcelain, with continued usage since the 18th century; also, the product of manufacturers and decorators who worked in the vicinity of Dresden in the 19th century.

*En cage:* Method of preparing a box so the corners are made of metal (such as gold) instead of the entire box.

Engraved designs: Designs of artists such as Watteau, Chardin and Boucher were rendered into engravings and then, as was the practice, painted on porcelain or made into porcelain figures.

Empire Style: Reign of Napoleon, 1799-1814.

*Enluminage:* Technique where a transfer print is on porcelain and a painter fills in the spaces between the outlines (on the transfer print).

*Fabrique par:* French for "made by." Sometimes found on the back of a box.

*Faience:* French adaptation of the name of the town of Faenza, the center for this craft, which began in the 15th century; also, earthenware with a glaze.

*Fait:* French for "done." Possible notation on the back of a box.

Feldspar: A variety of crystalline rocks which decomposed to form clay.

*Fleur-de-lys* or *fleur-de-lis:* Literally translated this means, flower of lily. A decorative, stylized heraldic symbol of three flowers bound together. The flower is considered to be a lily or iris flower, which was used by French rulers starting with Clovis I. The *fleur-de-lys* was also known as the flower of Louis. The iris/lily confusion was due to the belief at one point that the iris was in the category of lilies.

*Garnitures de Cheminee:* Decorative porcelain sets which were displayed on the fireplace mantel, originally consisting of seven, five or three pieces.

Genre: Term indicating paintings showing scenes from daily life.

Georgettes: Popular name for boxes made by goldsmith Jean George, who specialized in making ornamental boxes such as snuff boxes or *drageoirs*.

Glaze: Glassy coating applied to the surface of ceramics to render it impermeable to liquid. Glaze can be applied by dipping or spraying.

Glost: Second or glaze firing.

*Grand feu:* Decoration of porcelain fired at a high temperature.

*Grenade:* Motif of a bursting pomegranate.

*Gres:* French for stoneware.

*Grisaille:* Painting in shades of gray.

Grotesques or Grottesques: Fanciful designs, mixing animal and human forms and floral ornamentation, derived from decorations found in a Roman grotto, later identified as remains of Nero's palace. In the 18th century, they were referred to as arabesques.

*Guilloche:* Technique used on boxes and other items. *Boite a guilloche* was a box enhanced with machine engraving. Sometimes the engraving was done in wavy lines that look like moire. This could be enhanced with the addition of transparent enamel.

Hair receiver: At the turn of the century, hair left over from combing was used to augment hair styles, the hair receiver was the receptacle for this. The hair receiver was essentially a lidded box with a hole in the cover.

Harnessing: Over-all openwork design of box lid to hold hardstone work in place. The openwork could be in the form of tendriling foliage or other decorative motifs.

Hinge: The two types of box hinges are 1) Integral hinge—hinge hidden from view, used in 18th century French boxes; 2) stand away hinge—hinge with wide flange or rim that stands out from the box.

Honey gilding: Gilding technique that produced a soft, dull, rich finish; its ingredients included ground gold and honey (it sometimes had oil or lavender). A technique of gilding that followed, in the late 18th century, is *mercury gilding*. In mercury gilding, a combination of mercury and gold is applied to the piece and then fired. During the firing process, the mercury vaporizes and the piece is coated with the gold. The end product is brighter than honey gilding as well as cheaper and easier to produce.

Impressionist: Painting style started in the late 19th century. Haviland produced a line using Impressionistic techniques that met with little public acceptance. The line was discontinued.

Independent decorators: Hand painters of porcelain who worked outside the factory setting. In the 18th and 19th centuries, porcelain in the white was sometimes decorated off-site. In France, the term used in connection with this is *chamberlan* and in Germany the person is referred to as a *hausmaler*. Porcelain painting became a hobby at the turn of the century and home hand-painting continues to be done to this day.

*India or India goods:* Term used in 17th and 18th centuries to describe things imported from the Orient. It was probably due to the fact that the East India Company had a monopoly of trade with them.

Intaglio: Design carved into a surface; opposite of a cameo.

Japanese lacquer or Japanning: Japanese lacquer products were introduced into Europe in the 17th century. These items included boxes and other items. Japanning is the all inclusive term for lacquered products. Some of these products had as many as 50 coats of lacquer. (See also vernis Martin)

"Jeweled" porcelain: Enameling done, beginning about 1780, to simulate inlaid jewels; with translucent enamel over silver or gold foil made to imitate emeralds or rubies; opaque enamels appearing like turquoise or other opaque stones.

Kaolin: Hard clay which gives the porcelain item its whiteness and plasticity/malleability for modeling. Kaolin with quartz and feldspar, comprise the three essential components of hard paste porcelain.

Limoges enamels: Painted enamels used on boxes and other objects. In the 15th century, the term came to broadly include painted enamels of unknown origin.

*Limousin or Limousine:* From the area surrounding Limoges, the Limoges region of France; also, shepherd's cape.

*Louis Quatorze:* Louis XIV of France, reign 1643-1715.

*Louis Quinze:* Louis XV of France, reign 1715-1774.

*Louis Seize:* Louis XVI of France, reign 1774-1793.

*Maiolica:* Italian glazed earthenware.

*Majolica:* Victorian earthenware, introduced by Minton about 1850.

Melon fluting: Curved wave-like surface with an incised groove that has the overall appearance of a melon, initially used in silver to prevent denting.

Molds: Plaster forms introduced into potteries, circa 1775, into which liquid clay is poured and allowed to dry.

Monogram or Cipher of King used at Sevres: A monogram is a combination of two or more characters, symbols or letters into a design. The monogram of Louis XV is referred to interchangeably as intertwined, interlaced, interlocked or crossed Ls. Originally used on porcelain in 1753 at Vincennes. When used for hard paste at Sevres (from the discovery at Limoges until 1792) the royal cipher was usually surmounted by a crown and referred to as "Manufacture Royale." The mark is sometimes referred to as a cipher.

Neo-classical: Style begun in the mid-18th century in reaction to the finding of the ruins of Herculaneum and Pompeii, also referred to as *a l'antique* or *a la greeque.*

Nomenclature: The term used for an item within a category, e.g., *bonbonniere* or snuff box would be subsumed under the heading of boxes.

*Objet de vertu:* Small object of fine workmanship, artistry or luxury; hand decorated and constructed with costly materials.

*Oeil-de-perdrix:* French for "partridge eye." A design of a circle of dots with a central dot to break up a background color, like *cailloute.*

*Ormolu:* Term originating in the 18th century which literally means gilding with gold paste (*or moulu*); referred to as gilded bronze, gilt bronze or bronze dore.

Paste: The raw materials that make up porcelain. In stoneware and earthenware, the reference is body.

Pastilles: Small cones made of powdered charcoal, oils, perfumes, a binding agent and sometimes including powdered cinnamon.

*Pate Dure:* Hard paste.

*Pate sur pate:* Literally "paste on paste." A decorative technique in which a design is made by building up layers of slip; sometimes the technique entailed carving away slip. A thin application gives a semi-transparent effect. (If the slip is colored the technique is called *pate coloree.*) Louis Marc Solon, the most famous practitioner of this technique, used it at Sevres and Minton.

*Pate Tendre:* Soft paste.

*Peint et dore a la main:* French for "painted and gilded by hand." Back of box notation.

*Peinture fait main:* French for hand-painted. Back of box notation.

*Pietra-dura:* Italian art form consisting of inlaid marble and other stones such as lapis lazuli, agate, onyx, jasper and coral, made to form pictures. These pictures could include flowers, birds, and landscapes. While on the "grand tour," in the 17th and 18th century, the wealthy traveler purchased *pietra-dura* and sometimes had it made into boxes. Boxes were also made with micromosaics.

Pinchbeck: Metal with golden tone, invented by Christopher Pinchbeck (1670-1732), used in making snuff boxes in the 18th century.

Pomade pot: Small receptacle for pomade, a perfumed ointment with apple as an original ingredient.

Porcelain rooms: Rooms of royalty furnished in porcelain; including vases, figures, mirrors, furniture inlaid with plaques and other porcelain items.

*Porcelaine mousseline:* Fine, white, thin porcelain, initially made by J. Pouyat and then a Haviland designation. Possible back notation.

*Priser:* French word meaning "to take snuff" and also "to hold oneself in high regard."

Provenance: The origin (history or previous ownership) of a piece. Provenance can affect the price of a piece.

*Rehausse main:* French for "enhanced by hand." Back notation.

Renoir, Auguste: French Impressionist (1841-1919) who was born in Limoges. Some of his works are on display in Limoges.

Repairer: Employee in the porcelain factory who made sure the separate parts of elaborate figures were assembled and fired correctly.

*Repousse:* Technique used in metal snuff box making where the design is hammered from the back, resulting in a design in relief on front. In ceramics, the technique is done on wet clay which is pushed from the inside to change the surface.

Reserve: An area left white to receive decoration, such as flowers or scenes.

Rice grain: Particular porcelain technique in which porcelain is pierced and the resulting openings resemble grains of rice. The openings are then filled with glaze.

*Rococo:* Extension of Baroque with style becoming more delicate and asymmetrical. In France, the style is called Louis XV. It dates from about 1720 to 1760.

*Romanticism:* From the French for romance-like. In the 17th and 18th centuries, this term was used to indicate strange and unusual, as in a romance. Used to stress emotional and imaginative qualities.

*Rustic figuline:* Rustic earthenware, the root word "figulus" comes from the Latin word meaning potter and is a 16th century term used by Bernard Palissy for rustic ware. Also stands for pieces done in the manner of Palissy.

Samson: Samson, Edme and Co., 7 Rue Beranger, Paris from 1845. The firm that was the source of an enormous amount of fakes in porcelain and enamel objects.

Seal: Small device, with intaglio design, used in conjunction with sealing wax or paste.

Shagreen: Sturdy waterproof skin with grainy surface. From the 18th century forward, made from untanned sharkskin or fish skin (from the ray fish with the spines filed smooth), usually dyed green or black. Used as a covering for boxes. The term is also used for artificially produced pebbled leather; also, porcelain decorated in imitation of shagreen.

*Siecle de tabatiere:* French for "century of the snuffbox." Snuff boxes were fashionable for around 100 years, starting in the early-1700s.

*Singerie:* Designs using monkeys as a motif, seen as an exotic or frivolous element. Claude Audran III was considered the originator of the style. The style was also used by Berain in conjunction with arabesques and grotesques.

Slip: Liquid clay, about the consistency of cream, called *barbotine* in French. Used to attach separate parts of a ceramic composition to the body of the piece. Can be used to create relief decoration such as dots, lines or *pate sur pate.*

Snuff box cases, boxes or pouches: Some boxes had uneven surfaces due to elaborate workmanship and jewelling. These boxes were placed in protective cases made of shagreen, cloth, leather or other materials. Pouches were also used to keep the snuff box close to the body to keep the snuff warm.

Staffordshire: A famous pottery-producing region in England, which included the output of the factories located in Stoke on Trent, Burslem, Fenton, Hanley, Longton and Tunstall.

Sweetmeats: Sugary foods. The term came into being in 1456, when sugar was imported into England.

Tea caddy: Container for dry tea, often made in porcelain or pottery. Also known as tea canister or tea bottle.

Tea strainer: Small cup or handled cup with perforations for straining tea.

Thumbpiece or clasp: Slight projection on a snuff box or other objects, by which the lid is raised. The thumbpiece can be made in many shapes — a bud, leaf, etc. At the Louvre, one can see an 18th century porcelain box with a thumbpiece encrusted with diamonds. When a snuff box was for actual use rather than display, the thumbpiece and hinge mechanisms were as smooth as possible.

Tinder box: Small round or rectangular tin box which held tinder (and sometimes steel and flint) for lighting a candle or fire.

Tortoise shell: Shell obtained from the back of the Hawksbill turtle. Used in boxes for surface decoration or as an internal finishing technique. Tortoise shell, when heated, adheres to itself, thus needing no other adhesive.

Toy: Small metal box or cabinet, coming from English metal trade terminology. The word toy came from mispronouncing an archaic word "tigh" (and "tye"). The trade was referred to as "tye-making." Also, 18th century term for an expensive curiosity or amusing item for adults, such as a scent bottle, *etui,* snuff box, patch box, *breloque* (charm), seal, toothpick holder, etc.

Transfer: Engraved transfer printing as a process began in the 1750s. It originated at Battersea and was developed by John Brooks. The process entailed a number of steps. The first step was taking an engraved copper sheet, inking it with ceramic color and transferring it to tissue paper or thin pads made of gelatin or glue. (These thin pads were referred to as "bats.") While the design was still wet, it was pressed on to the porcelain surface, leaving an imprint. At this juncture the piece could be fired or if one desired, color could be added by hand (print and tint) and then the piece would be fired. This was cheaper and quicker than hand painting. Another method for transferring a pattern or design is by lithographic transfer (also known as decal). Lithographic transfer was invented in 1796 and used by the end of the 19th century. Using this process, the sheets of lithographic prints (or decals) are affixed to the ceramic body.

Treen: Miscellaneous small useful wooden objects for household or outside work purposes. Treen snuff boxes were sometimes lined with tortoise shell. The word "treen" means "of wood."

Trifle: Term meaning present, gift or souvenir, which went out of style in the 19th century.

*Trompe l' oeil:* Literally translated it means "to fool the eye." A technique employed in painting in which the image painted appears to be real. An example of this would be a porcelain box evoking the look of stone.

Trophy: Ornamental composition (painting or carving, etc.) showing symbolic montages of objects such as: drawing instruments, musical instruments, gardening tools, a bow and arrow, etc.

*Vaisseau a mat:* Stylized boat-shaped *pot pourri* container/table centerpiece.

Vernis Martin: French lacquer products made beginning in 1730 by Guillaume and Etienne Martin. They were designated "Manufacture Royale" and given the monopoly on japanned work in France. Snuff boxes and other objects were made using vernis Martin; in addition to black these items were made in green, gray, lilac, yellow and blue. The most famous was the green.

*Vertu* or *Virtu:* Term that indicates excellence or merit of fine arts, antique and curios.

Viands: Food products or delicacies.

Vitrification: Fusion of materials in porcelain which results in a hard, smooth, glassy finish.

Vitrine: Small cabinet, with a glass door and sides,for displaying treasured and fragile objects. Magnificent vitrines were made to specification for the wealthy collectors so boxes could be displayed on trays and still be protected.

Walking stick or cane head snuff box: Cane with a head incorporating a snuff box with a hinged cover, popular in the 18th century.

Wasters: Defective wares lost to sagging, crazing, warping, crackling, breakage, running of glaze or total collapse of the piece.

Wedgwood jasperware: Wedgwood company made many ceramic wares. Jasperware came into production in 1775. It has a dense stoneware body with an unglazed or biscuit surface. Wedgwood jasperware was the leader in neo-classical ceramics and was widely imitated. Snuff boxes were made using jasperware plaques.

Whites or blanks: Unpainted wares.

Zoophorus or zophorus: Classical frieze of relief sculptured figures of men or animals, or both, arranged continuously around a piece.

# Sources for Limoges Boxes

## Stores
### National Stores
#### California

| Gumps | Fine jewelry and gift stores |
|---|---|
| Neiman-Marcus | S & D |
| Nordstroms | Dubarry |

*Los Angeles area:*
Beverly Hills: Lucy Zahran & Co.
Costa Mesa: Lucy Zahran & Co.
Manhattan Beach: Lucy Zahran & Co., Coleman's Antiques
Rancho Palos Verdes: Morgan's Jewelers
Redondo Beach: MIXT (for Prince Charles related boxes)
Torrance: Melamed
San Fernando Valley: Grand Manner
Santa Barbara: P.S. Limited, Posh Jewelers
#### Connecticut
New Canaan: Sallea Antiques (Antique Boxes)
#### Louisiana
New Orleans: The Brass Monkey, Galleria Veronese, Lord Jim
#### Massachusetts
Andover: a' Limoges Antiques
Boston: Shreve, Crump & Low, La Ruche

#### New York
New York City: Scully & Scully, Florian Papp
#### France
Paris: Marechal

## Catalogs

| | |
|---|---|
| Barrons | Gumps |
| Bloomingdales | Horchow |
| Caprice | Ross Simon |
| Cashs of Ireland | Scully & Scully |
| Celebration Fantastic | Sugar Hill |
| Cottage Shop | Tiffany & Co. |
| Eximious/Limoges Encore | |

## Auction Houses

| | |
|---|---|
| Bonham | Phillips |
| Butterfield & Butterfield | Sotheby's |
| Christie's | |

## Internet
The Perfect Gift: www.limogesporcelainboxes.com

## Dealer
Debby DuBay of a' Limoges Antiques, Andover, Mass (featured in Victoria magazine's February 1997 article "Porcelain Paradise"). She has also been featured on Oprah.

## Newsletters or Periodicals

Antique & Collectors Reproduction News, in regard to
Antique Fakes  (P.O. Box 12130,
        Des Moines, IA 50312).
Dorothy Kamm's Porcelain Collector's Companion
        (P.O. Box 7460, Port Lucie, FL 34985)

## Venues for Viewing Boxes and Porcelain

*England (London)*
        Victoria & Albert Museum (Jewel Room,
            Wrightsman Collection) (Jones and Salting
            Collection)
        Wallace Collection (Sevres and others shown in
            room settings)
*France (Limoges)*
        Adrien Dubouche Museum (There is a book on
            Limoges porcelain available in English,
            entitled *The National Museum Adrien
            Dubouche*)
*France (Paris)*
        The Louvre
            (The Lenoir, Andre and Rothschild cases)
        Musee des Arts Decoratifs
            (The Schlichting collection)
        Le Musee de Cluny
        Musee du S.E.I.T.A. (Museum of Tobacco)
*France (Saint Yrieix la Perche)*
        Les Palloux
*France (Sevres)*
        Musee Ceramique of the Manufacture Nationale

*Germany*
        Hohenzollern Museum
*The Netherlands (Amsterdam)*
        Rijksmuseum
*Russia (Saint Petersburg)*
        Hermitage
*Switzerland (Geneva)*
        Museum of Art and History
*United States (California)*
        J. Paul Getty Museum (Los Angeles)
        Huntington Library & Gardens (San Marino)
*United States (Maryland)*
        Walters Art Gallery (Baltimore)
*United States (New York)*
        Metropolitan Museum of Art: (J. Pierpont Morgan
            Collection, Catherine Wentworth Collection,
            Linsky Collection) (New York City)
        Cooper-Hewitt Museum, The Smithsonian
            Institution's National Museum of Design
            (New York City)
*United States (Washington, D.C.)*
        Hillwood Museum

## Ceramic Fairs

*England (London)*
        International Ceramic Fair and Seminar

*France (Paris)*
Association des Specialistes de Ceramique de
    Collection

# Manufacturers' Marks

Marks on porcelain come in many guises. They can serve to identify workers or factories. The worker indicated could be a painter, gilder, glazer, designer, joiner or person who forms the piece. The mark could also indicate the name of the factory, expressed in letters or symbols. There are variations in applying the mark, it can be: stamped (impressed), painted, stenciled, incised or printed.

## Warning About Marks

There are a number of factors in relation to marks and porcelain that make this area a morass of problems. First, early snuff boxes were seldom marked; it has been suggested that a mark on the bottom of the box would have been aesthetically contraindicated. Secondly, manufacturers were derivative of one another. Some factories produced outright copies of designs with marks that approximated marks from more famous or desirable factories. Another confusing factor was that workers in porcelain moved from factory to factory. It is understandable why it is difficult to attribute an early porcelain piece to a specific factory or town.

To this day marks are variable. After 1891, the word "France" may be found on pieces of Limoges porcelain imported into the United States. This is due to the McKinley Tariff Act. Prior to that, the back marking could be variable, listing the city or other marks. After 1914, the words "Made in" may be marked on some boxes.

Marks can be used to help in some fashion, but they should not be used as a defining source. As stated by Cox in *The Book of Pottery and Porcelain* in 1946: "Marks cannot be trusted." Given all these caveats:

*Books with listings of French porcelain marks*
        d' Albis, Meslin-Perrier, Danckert, Haggar, Auscher, Litchfield, Honey, Savage, Cox, Chaffers, Hughes (G.B.), Travis, Gaston, plus others. Regrettably, many sources for French porcelain marks are available primarily in Europe.

*New factories*
        Akil, Carpenet, French Accents, Parry-Vielle, Porcelaine Faye et Fils, Legle Legrand Lebouc, Site Corot and Le Trefle.

## The Marks

 **Ancienne Manufacture Royale**

hand-painted

(whites)
**Artoria**

 **Bernardaud plus others**

 **Carpenet**

 **Chamart/Charles Martine plus others**

 **Chanille**

 **Dubarry/ Porcelaine de Limoges**

 **Fabergé**

 **Faye Et Fils**

 **FD Limoges**

 **Fontanille & Marraud**

  **French Accents**

 **HAVILAND** **Haviland/Castel**

 **Jammet Seignolles**

 **La Gloriette**

 **La Seynie**

 **Le Trefle**

 **Porc. Leclair**

 **Legle Legrand Lebouc**

 **Manufacture Nouvelle de Porcelaine**

 **Parry Vieille**

 **Prevot**

 **Raynaud et Cie**

 **RCM**

 **Rochard/plus others**

 **Royal Limoges**

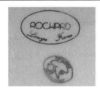 **S&D Collectibles**

  **Site Corot**

**167**

# Bibliography

## Magazines & Newspapers

Ashford, Roger, "English Vesta Boxes," *The Antiques Journal*, September 1979, pp. 28-29, 49.

Askew, Richard B.M., "Elegant Snuffboxes of the 17th and 18th Centuries," *Spinning Wheel*, September 1971, pp. 52-53.

Benton, Eric, "English Painted Enamel Toys of the 18th Century," *Virginia Museum*, Vol. 14, No. 2, Winter 1974.

Bernier, Olivier, "Napoleon's Grand Designs," *House & Garden*, December 1987, pp. 146-151, 208-210.

Blonston, Gary, "A Surprise in Every Box," *Art & Antiques*, February 1995, pp. 74-77.

Burton, Marda, "Masterworks: Versailles in Mississippi," *Veranda*, Spring 1998, pp. 32-42.

Cruikshank, Jan, "Haviland: An American Family Tradition," *West Coast Peddler*, April 1999, pp. cover, 49, 51-52, 54-56.

Deitz, Paula, "Decorative Boxes House Secrets and Surprises," *New York Times*, August 27, 1989, p. 32.

Doversberger, Robert, "The Havilands," *Haviland Collectors Internationale Foundation*, Vol. 7, No. 2, September 1996, p 3.

Fourest, Henry-Pierre, "French Soft-Paste Snuffboxes at Limoges," *Antiques*, May 1961, pp. 455-457.

Fredgant, Don, "William Lycett: Atlanta's China Painter," *The Antiques Journal*, March 1981, pp. 16-19, 44-45.

Gaston, Mary Frank, "Limoges Porcelain," *The Antique Trader*, Vol. XVII, No. 2, Issue No. 64, April 1986, pp. 21-25.

Hamm, Larry, "The History of Charles Field Haviland and GDA," *Haviland Collectors Internationale Foundation*, Vol. 9, No. 2, September 1998, pp. 4-5.

Hogan, E.P., "Collectible Silverplate Jewel Caskets of Long Ago," *Spinning Wheel*, September 1971, pp. 10-11.

Honey, W.B., "European Porcelain of the Eighteenth Century," *Antiques*, March 1962, pp. 316-319.

Husfloen, Kyle, "Collectible Sugar Bowls," *The Antique Trader Weekly*, Vol. XVI, No. 4, Issue No. 60, August 1985, p 90.

Kamm, Dorothy, "American Painted Porcelain," *Antique Trader's Collector Magazine & Price Guide*, May 1997.

Kamm, Dorothy, "Little Chubby Cherubs Charm China Collectors," *Haviland Collectors Internationale Foundation*, Vol. 9, No. 1, July, 1998, pp. 10.

Keefer, John Webster, "In New Orleans: Old Paris Porcelain, *Veranda*, Spring 1998, pp. 272b-272n.

Koenenn, Connie, "A Soft Touch," *Los Angeles Times*, November 7, 1997, pp. 1-2.

Lindquist, David, "The Grand Scam," *Southern Accents*, November/December 1997, pp. 66-72.

McClinton, Katherine Morrison, "American Hand-painted China," *Spinning Wheel*, April 1967, pp. 10-12, 43.

McClinton, Katherine Morrison, "English and American Miniature Pottery," *Hobbies*, June 1984, pp. 18-22.

McKinley, Cameron Curtis, "The Artistry of Fine Porcelain," *Architectural Digest*, December 1981, pp. 172-180.

Moehlman, Ruth, "Intriguing Snuff Boxes of the Late 18th & 19th Century," *Hobbies: The Magazine for Collectors*, March 1984, pp. 96-98.

Norton, Martin, "Gold Snuff Boxes of the XVIIIth Century," *Apollo*, Vol. XXXV, 1942, pp. 25-27, 50-53, 72.

Poese, Bill, "Chatelaines," *The Antiques Journal*, June 1976, pp. 30-31, 50.

"Porcelain Paradise: Debby DuBay's Collection and Store," *Victoria*, February 1997, pp. 94-97.

Ray, Marcia, "A, B, C's of Ceramics," *Spinning Wheel*, November 1967, pp. 16-17.

Rivera, Betty and Ted, "Inkstands and Inkwells," *The Antiques Journal*, November 1979, p 16-19.

Sanders, Deborah Merck, "Table Manners: Bravo! at Bernardaud," *Veranda*, Spring 1998, pp. 46-62.

Schneider, Mike, "Porcelain a la France," *Antiques & Collecting*, May 1988, pp. 46-48, 51-52.

Tait, Hugh, "Eighteenth-Century Gold Boxes," *The Connoisseur*, December 1963, pp. 216-225.

Titus, Karen, "The Legacy of Limoges Boxes," *Romantic Homes*, September 1995, premier issue, pg. 16.

Tindall, Gillian, "The Country Airs and Graces of Limoges," *The New York Times*, March 10,1996, Travel Section, pg. 9.

Tjossem, Morla W., "Pickard China: Art for the Carriage Trade," *Antique Journal*, August 1980, p.12-17, 43-44.

Tjossem, Morla W., "Through the Eyes of a China Mender: How to Detect Repairs," *The Antiques Journal*, March 1980, pp. 32-33, 52-53.

Van Patten, Joan, "Nippon and Noritake: Home-decorated pieces can be identified by shapes," *Schroeder's Insider*, February 1985. (French forms shown)

Victoria Magazine, "Porcelain Paradise, Debby DuBay's Collection and Store," *Victoria*, February 1997, pp. 94-97.

Ward, Bradley, "For Dippers & Sniffers Only!", *Yankee*, February 1969.

Whittemore, Edwin C., "Sniff Boxes and Spittle Cups," *Spinning Wheel*, April 1967, p 24.

Williams, Ericka., "Did You Know There is no Such Thing as Dresden China," *Porcelain Artist*, March/April 1992, pp. 46-47.

## Books (various contributors)

*Discovering Antiques: The Story of World Antiques*, Greyston (New York, NY: 1972).

*The Encyclopedia of Collectibles*, Time-Life (Virginia: 1980).

*L'Art de Vivre*: Decorative Arts and Design in France 1789-1989, Vendome Press/Cooper-Hewitt Museum (New York, NY: 1989).

*World Antiques*, Hazel Harrison, ed., Chartwell Books, Inc. (Secaucus, NJ: 1978).

## Books (compilations)

Atterbury, Paul, ed., *The History of Porcelain*, William Morrow & Co., Inc. (New York, NY: 1982).

Battie, David, ed., *Sotheby's Concise Encyclopedia of Porcelain*, Little, Brown & Co. (London: 1990).

Burchfield, R.W., ed., *The Oxford English Dictionary*, Clarendon Press (Oxford: 1989).

Constable, George, ed., *France*, Time-Life Books, Inc. (Amsterdam: 1984).

Charleston, Robert J., ed., *World Ceramics*, Hamlyn (New York, NY: 1971).

Edwards, Ralph and L.G.G. Ramsey, editors, *The Connoisseur's Complete Periods Guides*, Bonanza Books (New York, NY: 1968).

Hayward, Helena, ed., *The Connoisseur's Handbook of Antique Collecting*, Galahad Book (New York, NY: 1960).

O'Neill, John P., ed., *The Jack and Belle Linsky Collection in the Metropolitan Museum of Art*, The Metropolitan Museum of Art (New York, NY: 1984).

Osborne, Harold, ed., *The Oxford Companion to Art*, Oxford at the Clarendon Press (Oxford: 1979).

Phillips, Phoebe, ed., *The Collector's Encyclopedia of Antiques*, Crown Publishers, Inc. (1973).

Ramsey, L.G.G., ed., *The Complete Encyclopedia of Antiques*, Hawthorn Books (New York, NY: 1967).

Ramsey, L.G.G., ed., *The Complete Color Encyclopedia of Antiques*, revised and expanded edition, Hawthorn Books (New York, NY: 1975).

Runes, Dagobert D. and Harry G Schrickel, ed., *Encyclopedia of the Arts*, Philosophical Library (New York, NY: 1946).

Turner, Jane, ed., *The Dictionary of Art*, Grove's Dictionaries Inc. (New York, NY: 1996).

## Books

d'Albis, Jean, translation to English by Laurens d'Albis, *Haviland*, Dessain et Tolra (Paris: 1988).

d'Albis, Jean and Celeste Romanet, *La Porcelaine de Limoges*, Sous Le Vent (Paris: 1980).

Aldridge, Eileen, *Porcelain*, Grosset & Dunlap (New York, NY: 1970).

Andere, Mary, *Old Needlework Boxes and Tools: Their Story and How to Collect Them*, Drake Publishers Ltd. (New York, NY: 1971).

Arnau, Frank (pseud), Schmitt, Heinrich, *The Art of the Faker: Three Thousand Years of Deceptions*, Little, Brown & Co. (Boston: 1961).

Auscher, Ernest Simon, translated and edited by William Burton, *A History and Description of French Porcelain*, Cassell and Co., Ltd. (London: 1905).

Avery, C. Louise, *Masterpieces of European Porcelain*, Metropolitan Museum of Art (New York, NY: 1949).

Bacci, Mina, *European Porcelain*, Paul Hamlyn, translated from Italian (London: 1969).

Banister, Judith, *English Silver*, Hamlyn Publications (London: 1966).

Barber, Edwin Atlee, *The Ceramic Collectors' Glossary*, Da Capro Press (New York, NY: 1967).

Beaucamp-Markowsky, Barbara, *Boites En Porcelaine*, Office de Livre S.A. (Switzerland: 1985).

Beaucamp-Markowsky, Barbara, *Collection of 18th Century Porcelain Boxes*, Rijksmuseum, (Amsterdam: 1988).

Bedford, John, *All Kinds of Small Boxes*, Walker and Co. (New York, NY: 1966).

Bedford, John, *Talking About Teapots*, Max Parrish & Co. (London: 1964).

Berges, Ruth, *The Collector's Cabinet*, A.S. Barnes & Company, Inc. (London: 1980).

Berges, Ruth, *From Gold to Porcelain: The Art of Porcelain and Faience*, Thomas Yoseloff (New York, NY: 1963).

Berry-Hill, Henry and Sidney, *Antique Gold Boxes*, Aberlard Press (New York, NY: 1953).

Benjamin, Susan, *English Enamel Boxes From the Eighteenth to the Twentieth Centuries*, Little, Brown (England: 1993).

Benjamin, Susan, *The First 25 Years of Halcyon Days Enamels*, Benjamin Dent & Co. (London: 1995).

Bernier, Olivier, *The Eighteenth-Century Woman*, Doubleday & Co., NY, published in association with The Metropolitan Museum of Art (New York, NY: 1981).

Bernier, Olivier, *Louis XIV: A Royal Life*, Doubleday (New York, NY: 1987).

Blade, Timothy Trent, *Antique Collecting*, Iowa State University Press (Ames, Iowa: 1989).

Blakemore, Kenneth, *Snuff Boxes*, Frederick Muller Ltd. (London: 1976).

Boger, Louise Ade, *House and Gardens Antiques: Questions and Answers*, Simon & Schuster (New York, NY: 1973).

Boger, Louise Ade and H. Batterson Boger, *The Dictionary of Antiques and the Decorative Arts*, Charles Scribner's Sons (New York, NY: 1967).

Bosomworth, Dorothy/Intro., *The Victorian Catalogue of Household Goods*, Studio Editions (London: 1993) first published in 1883 under a different title.

Burgess, Anthony and Francis Haskell, *The Age of the Grand Tour*, Crown Publishers, Inc. (New York, NY: 1967).

Canaday, John, *Metropolitan Seminars in Art: The Artist as a Social Critic*, The Metropolitan Museum of Art (1959).

Caroselli, Susan L., *The Painted Enamels of Limoges*, Los Angeles County Museum of Art (Los Angeles, CA: 1993).

Charles, Rollo, *Continental Porcelain of the 18th Century*, Ernest Benn Limited (London: 1964).

Chaffers, William, *Concise Marks & Monograms*, Wordsworth Editions (England: 1988).

Chefetz, Sheila, *Antiques for the Table*, Penguin Studio Books (New York, NY: 1993).

Chefetz, Sheila, *Modern Antiques for the Table*, Penguin Studio Books (New York, NY: 1998).

Clemens, Samuel L., *A Tramp Abroad*, Scholarly Press (Michigan: 1968).

Cole, Brian, *Boxes*, Chilton Book Company (Radnor, PA: 1976).

Costantino, Ruth, *How to Know French Antiques*, Clarkson N. Potter, Inc. (New York, NY: 1961).

Constable, W.G., *Collectors and Collecting*, Art Treasures of the World (New York, NY: 1954).

Cowie, Donald and Keith Henshaw, *Antique Collector's Dictionary*, Gramercy Publishing Co. (New York, NY: 1962).

Cox, Warren E., *The Book of Pottery and Porcelain*, Vol. II, Crown Publishers, Inc. (New York, NY: 1946).

"The Crystal Palace Exhibition, Illustrated Catalogue, London," The Art-Journal (London: 1851); reprint, Dover Publications (New York, NY: 1970).

Cunynghame, Henry H., *European Enamels*, G.P. Putnum's Sons (London: 1906).

Curtis, Mattoon M., *The Book of Snuff and Snuff Boxes*, Liveright Publishing Corp. (New York, NY: 1935).

Cushion, John Patrick, *Animals in Pottery and Porcelain*, Crown Publishers, Inc. (New York, NY: 1974).

Cushion, John Patrick, *Continental China Collecting for Amateurs*, Frederick Muller (London: 1970).

Cushion, John Patrick, *Pottery & Porcelain Tablewares*, William Morrow & Co., Inc. (New York, NY: 1976).

Danckert, Ludwig, *Manuel de la Porcelaine Europeenne*, Bibliotheque des Arts (Paris: 1980).

Darling, Ada W., *The Jeweled Trail: Collecting Antique Jewelry*, Wallace-Homestead Book Co., (Des Moines, Iowa: 1971).

Dauterman, Carl Christian, *Sevres*, Walker and Co. (New York, NY: 1969).

Davis, Frank, Walter de Sager, Kenneth Blakemore & others, *Antiques*, Octopus Books (London: 1978).

Dawes, Nicholas M., *Majolica*, Crown Publishers, Inc. (New York, NY: 1990).

DeForrest, Michael, *Antiquing From A to Z*, Simon and Schuster (New York, NY: 1975).

Delieb, Eric, *Investing in Silver*, Clarkson N. Potter, Inc. (New York, NY: 1967).

Delieb, Eric, *Silver Boxes*, Exeter Books (New York, NY: 1979).

Detweiler, Susan Gray, *George Washington's Chinaware*, Harry N. Abrams, Inc. (New York, NY: 1982).

Dorn, Sylvia O'Neill, *The Insider's Guide to Antiques, Art and Collectibles*, Doubleday & Company, Inc. (New York, NY: 1974).

Druitt, Silvia, *Antique Personal Possessions*, Blandford Press (Poole, England: 1980).

Drury, Elizabeth, *Antiques (Traditional techniques of the master crafts-men: furniture, glass, ceramics, gold, silver and much more)*, Bloomsbury Books (London: 1992).

DuCann, C.G.L., *Antiques for Amateurs*, Barnes & Noble (New York, NY: 1969).

Duff, Gail, *A Book of Pot-Pourri*, Beaufort Books (New York, NY: 1985).

Dynes, Wayne, *Palaces of Europe*, Paul Hamlyn Publishing, (Feltham, Middlesex, England: 1968).

Eberlein, Harold Donaldson and Roger Wearne Ramsdell, *The Practical Book of Chinaware*, Halcyon House (Gordon City, NY, 1925 2nd edition, 1942).

Feild, Rachael, *Macdonald Guide to Buying Antique Pottery & Porcelain*, Wallace-Homestead Book Co. (Radnor, PA: 1987).

Fisher, Stanley W., *Fine Porcelain & Pottery*, Galahad Books (New York, NY: 1974).

Flack, Audrey, *Art & Soul*, E.P. Dutton (New York, NY: 1986).

Gaston, Mary Frank, *The Collector's Encyclopedia of Limoges Porcelain*, Collector Books, Division of Schroeder Publishing Co. (Paducah, KY: 1980, 1st ed.; 1992, 2nd ed.; 1996, updated values).

Gaston, Mary Frank, *Haviland Collectables and Ojects of Art*, Collector Books, Division of Schroeder Publishing Co. (Paducah, Kentucky: 1984).

Gauthier, Marie-Madeleine and Madeleine Marcheix and W. & B. Forman, *Limoges Enamels*, Paul Hamlyn (London: 1962).

Gauthier, Maximilian, *The Louvre: Sculpture, Ceramics, Objets d' Art*, Appleton-Century (New York, NY: 1964).

Gendler, Ruth J., *The Book of Qualities*, Perennial Library (New York, NY: 1988).

Gerson, Roselyn, *Ladies' Compacts*, Wallace-Homestead Book Co. (Radnor, PA: 1989).

Gilliatt, Mary, *The Mary Gilliatt Book of Color*, Little, Brown & Co. (Boston: 1986).

Gloag, John, *A Social History of Furniture Design*, Crown Publishers, Inc. (New York, NY: 1966).

Godden, Geoffrey A., *Antique Glass & China: A Guide for the Beginning Collector*, A.S. Barnes & Co. (Cranbury, NY: 1966).

Gohm, Douglas, *Small Antiques for the Collector*, Arco Publishing Co., Inc. (New York, NY: 1968).

Goldenberg, Rose Leiman, *Antique Jewelry*, Crown Publishers, Inc. (New York, NY: 1976).

de Goncourt, Edmond and Jules, *French Eighteenth-Century Painters*, first published by Phaidon Press in 1948; rev. ed. by Cornell University Press (Ithaca, NY: 1981).

Gonzalez-Palacios, Alvar, *The Age of Louis XV*, Paul Hamlyn (London: 1969).

Gonzalez-Palacios, Alvar, *The Age of Louis XVI*, Paul Hamlyn (London: 1969).

Gump, Richard, *Good Taste Costs No More*, Doubleday & Co. (New York, NY: 1951).

Habsburg-Lothringen, Geza von, *Gold Boxes from the Collection of Rosalinde and Arthur Gilbert*, self-published: 1983).

Haggar, Reginald George, *The Concise Encyclopedia of Continental Pottery & Porcelain*, Andre Deutsch (London: 1960).

Hannover, Emil, edited by Bernard Rackham, *Pottery & Porcelain, Vol. III, European Porcelain*, translated from Danish, Ernest Benn Ltd. (London: 1925).

Harris, Nathaniel, *Porcelain Figurines*, Golden Press (New York, NY: 1974).

Havard, Henry, *La Ceramique (Fabrication)*, Librairie Charles Delagrave, (Paris: c1890)

Henderson, Marjorie and Elizabeth Wilkinson, *Whatnot*, William Morrow and Co. (London: 1977).

Hickman, Peggy, *Silhouettes*, Walker and Co. (NY: 1968).

Hillier, Bevis, *The Social History of the Decorative Arts—Pottery and Porcelain, 1700-1914*, Meredith Press (NY: 1968).

Hogg, Min, Wendy Harroop and the World of Interiors, *Interiors*, Clarkson Potter Inc. (NY 1988).

Honey, William Boyer, *Dresden China*, Tudor Publ. Co. (NY: 1946).

Honey, William Boyer, *European Ceramic Art from the end of the Middle Ages to about 1815*, Faber and Faber Limited, (London 1952)

Honey, William Boyer, *French Porcelain of the 18th Century*, 2nd ed., Faber and Faber (London: 1972).

Hughes, Bernard G., *English Snuff Boxes*, MacGibbon & Kee (London: 1971).

Hughes, Bernard G., *Pocket Book of China*, Country Life (London: 1977).

Hughes, Bernard G., *Small Antique Silverware*, Bramhall House (New York, NY: 1957).

Hughes, Therle, *Antiques: An Illustrated A-Z*, World Publishing Co. (1972).

Hughes, Therle, *Small Antiques for the Collector*, Macmillan Co. (New York, NY: 1964).

Imber, Diana, *Collecting European Delft and Faience*, Frederick A. Praeger (New York, NY: 1968).

Ingamells, John, *The Wallace Collection*, Scala Books (rev. ed., London: 1994).

Jackson, Mary L., *If Dishes Could Talk: The History & Romance of Old China*, Wallace-Homestead Book Co. (2nd rev. ed., Des Moines, IA: 1971).

Jenkins, Emyl, *Appraisal Book*, Three Rivers Press (New York, NY: 1995).

Jenkins, Dorothy H., *The Woman's Day Book of Antique Collectibles*, Citadel Press (Secaucus, NJ: 1982).

Johnston, Susanna, *Collecting: The Passionate Pastime*, Harper & Row (New York, NY: 1986).

Kamm, Dorothy, *American Painted Porcelain*, Antique Trader Books (Norfolk, VA: 1999).

Kamm, Dorothy, *American Painted Porcelain: Collector's Identification & Value Guide*, Collector Books, Division of Schroeder Publishing Co. (Paducah, KY: 1997).

Karmason, Marilyn G. and Joan B. Stacke, *Majolica*, Harry N. Abrams, Inc. (New York, NY: 1989).

Katzander, Howard L., *Antiques and Art: How to Know, Buy and Use Them*, Doubleday & Co., Inc. (New York, NY: 1977).

Kelley, Austin P., *The Anatomy of Antiques*, Viking Press (New York, NY: 1974).

Ketchum, William C., *Boxes*, Cooper-Hewitt Museum, Smithsonian Institution (1982).

Klamkin, Marian, *The Collector's Book of Boxes*, Dodd, Mead & Co. (New York, NY: 1970).

Kovel, Ralph and Terry, *Know Your Antiques*, Crown Publishers, Inc. (New York, NY: 1967).

Landais, Hubert, *French Porcelain: Pleasures and Treasures*, G.P. Putnam's Sons (New York, NY: 1961).

Lahaussois, Christine, *Animaux-Boites Porcelaine*, Musee Des Arts Decoratifs, (Tours 1992).

Latham, Jean, *Collecting Miniature Antiques*, Charles Scribner's (New York, NY: 1972).

Latham, Jean, *Victoriana: A Guide for Collectors*, Stein & Day Publishers (New York, NY: 1971).

Laver, James, *The Age of Illusion: Manners and Morals 1750-1848*, David McKay Co., Inc. (New York, NY: 1972).

Le Corbeiller, Clare, *European and American Snuff Boxes: 1730-1830*, Viking Press (1966); Chancellor Press (London: 1983).

Lee, Ruth Webb, *Antiques, Fakes and Reproductions* (Framingham Center, MA: 1938).

Lewis, Philippa and Gillian Darley, *Dictionary of Ornament*, Pantheon Books (New York, NY: 1986).

Litchfield, Frederick, *Pottery and Porcelain: A Guide to Collectors*, 6th ed., revised by Frank Tilley, Adam and Charles Black (London: 1953).

Mackay, James, *An Encyclopedia of Small Antiques*, Harper & Row (New York, NY: 1975).

Mankowitz, Wolf, *Wedgwood*, Spring Books (London: 1966), first published by B.T. Batsford Ltd. in 1953.

Manroe, Candace Ord, *Designing with Collectibles*, Simon & Schuster, Michael Friedman Group (New York, NY: 1992).

Marion, John L., *The Best of Everything*, Simon and Schuster (New York, NY: 1989).

Marryat, Joseph, *A History of Pottery and Porcelain*, William Clowes and Sons, 2nd ed., (London: 1857).

McCausland, Hugh, *Snuff & Snuff Boxes*, The Batchworth Press (London: 1951).

McClinton, Katherine Morrison, *The Complete Book of Small Antique Collecting*, Cowan-McCann, Inc. (New York, NY: 1965).

Meslin-Perrier, Chantal, *Chefs-d'oeuvre de la Porcelaine de Limoges*, Reunion des Musees Nationaux (Paris: 1996).

Meslin-Perrier, Chantal, *The National Museum Adrien Dubouche: Limoges*, Reunion des Musees Nationaux (Paris: no date).

Mills, John Fitzmaurice, *How to Detect Fake Antiques*, Desmond Elliott Publishing (New York, NY: 1980).

Morley-Fletcher, Hugo, *Meissen Porcelain in Color*, Exeter Books (New York, NY: 1979).

Montague, Prosper, *Larousse Gastronomique*, Crown Publishers (NY: 1961).

Moss, Charlotte, *A Passion for Detail*, Doubleday (New York, NY: 1991).

Mullenix, Dennis, *Antiques: A Browser's Handbook*, Harper & Row (New York, NY: 1977).

Newman, Harold, *Veilleuses, A Definitive Review of Ceramic Food and Tea Warmers*, A.S. Barnes and Company (South Brunswick, NJ: 1967).

Nocq, Henry et Carle Dreyfus, *Tabatieres, Boites et Etuis*, G. Van Oest (Paris, 1930).

O'Gorman, Joseph, F., *Limoges: Its People, Its China*, Bawo & Dotter (New York, NY: 1900).

Ohrbach, Barbara Milo, *Antiques at Home*, Clarkson N. Potter Inc. (New York, NY: 1989).

Oldenbourg, Zoe, *Catherine the Great*, translated from French, Pantheon Books (1965).

Patterson, Jerry E., *Porcelain*, Cooper-Hewitt Museum, Smithsonian Institution (1979).

Payton, Mary and Geoffrey, *The Observer's Book of Pottery and Porcelain*, Frederick Warne (London: 1981).

Pearon, Katherine, *Accent on Accessories*, Editorial Director, Oxmoor

House (Birmingham, AL: 1995).

Pearsall, Ronald, *Illustrated Guide to Collecting Antiques*, Smithmark (New York, NY: 1996).

Pearsall, Ronald, *The Joy of Antiques*, David & Charles (London: 1989).

Perrier, Antoine, *Porcelaines de Limoges*, Dessins de Jean Virolle (Limoges, France: 1937).

Perry, Evan, *Collecting Antique Metalware*, Doubleday & Co. (New York, NY: 1974).

Pinot de Villechenon, Marie-Noelle, translated by John Gilbert, *Sevres: Porcelain from the Sevres Museum 1740 to the Present Day*, Lund Humphries Publishers (London: 1997).

Pinto, Edward H., *Treen or Small Woodware Throughout the Ages*, B.T. Batsford Ltd. (London: 1949).

de Plas, Solange, *Tabatieres*, Editions Ch. Massin (Paris: no date).

Plinval de Guillebon, Regine de, *Porcelain of Paris: 1770-1850*, translated by Robin R. Charleston, Walker and Co. (New York, NY: 1972).

Pope-Hennessy, John, *The Random House Encyclopedia of Antiques*, Random House (New York, NY: 1973).

Ray, Marcia, *Collectible Ceramics*, Crown Publishers, Inc. (New York, NY: 1974).

Revi, Albert Christian, *Spinning Wheel's Antiques for Women*, Castle Books (PA: 1974).

Reynolds, Ernest, *Guide to European Antiques*, A.S. Barnes and Co., Inc. (New York, NY: 1964).

Richter, Detley, *Lacquered Boxes*, Schiffer (PA: 1989).

Ricketts, Howard, *Objects of Vertue*, Barrie & Jenkins (1971); also published as Ricketts, Howard, *Antique Gold & Enamelware*, Doubleday & Co. (NJ: 1971).

Riley, Noel, *Tea Caddies*, first published with Lutterworth Press (Cambridge, England: 1985); published in United States, Seven Hills Books (Cincinnati, OH: 1985).

Roe, F. Gordon, *Home Furnishing with Antiques*, Hastings House (New York, NY: 1965).

Rogers, Frances and Alice Beard, *5,000 Years of Gems and Jewelry*, J.B. Lippincott Co. (Philadelphia and New York: 1947).

Rogers, Gay Ann, *An Illustrated History of Needlework Tools*, John Murray Ltd. (London: 1983).

Rollins, Alice R., *Antiques for the Home*, Harper and Bros. Publishing (New York, NY: 1946).

Rosenblum, Robert, *Transformations in Late Eighteenth Century Art*, third printing, Princeton University Press (Princeton, NJ: 1974).

Ross, Pat, *To Have and to Hold: Decorative American Boxes*, Viking (New York, NY: 1991).

Rottgen, Steffi and Alvar Gonzales-Palacio, *The Art of Mosaics*, Los Angeles County Museum of Art, rev. ed. (Los Angeles, CA: 1982).

Rust, Gordon A., *Collector's Guide to Antique Porcelain*, Viking (New York, NY: 1973).

Rybczynski, Witold, *Home: A Short History of an Idea*, Viking (New York, NY: 1986).

Sandon, John, *Antique Porcelain*, Antique Collectors' Club (Woodbridge, Suffolk: 1997).

Sandon, Henry, *Coffee Pots and Tea Pots for the Collector*, Arco Publishing Co., Inc. (New York, NY: 1974).

Savage, George, *The Antique Collector's Handbook*, The Hamlyn Publishing Group (London: 1971), 1st ed., 1959.

Savage, George, *Ceramics for the Collector: An Introduction to Pottery and Porcelain*, Rockiff (London: 1955).

Savage, George, *Dictionary of Antiques*, Praeger Publishers (New York, NY: 1970).

Savage, George, *Dictionary of 19th Century Antiques*, G.P. Putnam's Sons (New York, NY: 1979).

Savage, George, *French Decorative Art: 1638-1793*, Frederick A. Praeger (New York, NY: 1969).

Savage, George, *Porcelain Through the Ages*, Penguin Books (Baltimore, MD: 1963).

Savage, George, *Seventeenth and Eighteenth Century French Porcelain*, MacMillan (New York, NY: 1960).

Savage, George and Harold Newman, *An Illustrated Dictionary of Ceramics*, Thames and Hudson (London: 1985).

Savill, Rosalind, *Wallace Collection: Sevres Porcelain*, 2nd ed., The Trustees of the Wallace Collection (London: 1980).

Schmidt, Robert, translated by W.A. Thorpe, *Porcelain as an Art and a Mirror of Fashion*, George G. Harrap and Company, Ltd. (London: 1932).

Schneider, Bruno F., *Renoir*, Crown Publishers, Inc. (New York, NY: 1958).

Smith, Allan B. and Helen B. Smith, *840 Individual Open Salts Illustrated, The Seventh Book*, The Country House (Topsham, ME: 1980).

Smith, Allan B. and Helen B. Smith, *1,334 Open Salts Illustrated, The Tenth Book*, The Country House (Topsham, ME: 1984).

Smith, Allan B. and Helen B. Smith and Daniel M Snyder, *1,100 Open Salts Illustrated, Individuals and Masters, The Eighth Book*, The Country House (Topsham, ME: 1981).

Snowman, A. Kenneth, *Eighteenth Century Gold Boxes of Europe*, Antique Collectors' Club (1990).

Snowman, A. Kenneth, *Eighteenth Century Gold Boxes of Europe*, Faber And Faber (London: 1966).

Stewart, Sidney, *How to Know and Buy French Antiques*, A. Romand et M. Beurel (Paris: 1953).

Stuart, Sheila, *Small Antiques for the Small Home*, A.S. Barne's and Co. (New York, NY: 1968).

Tait, Hugh, *Porcelain*, Marboro Books (New York, NY: 1962).

Tallis, David, *Music Boxes: A Guide for Collectors*, Stein and Day (New York, NY: 1971).

Tomasini, Wallace J., *Celebrating 150 Years of Haviland China: 1842-1992*, Haviland Collectors International (1992).

Trager, James, *The Food Chronology*, Henry Holt and Company (New York, NY: 1995).

Travis, Nora, *Haviland China: The Age of Elegance*, Schiffer Publications Ltd. (PA.: 1997).

Trimble, Alberta C., *Modern Porcelain: Today's Treasures Tomorrow's Traditions*, Harper & Brothers Publishers (New York, NY: 1962).

Verrill, A. Hyatt, *Perfumes and Spices*, L.C. Page and Co. (Boston: 1940).

Walkling, Gillan, *Tea Caddies: An Illustrated History*, Victoria and Albert Museum, (1985).

Wardell-Yerburgh, J.C., *The Pleasure of Antiques*, Octopus Books (London: 1974).

Watson, Lucilla, *Understanding Antiques*, Viking (New York, NY: 1987).

Weaver, Gabrielle, edited, *Antiques in the Home*, Marshall Cavendish (London: 1974).

Wheldon, Keith, *Renoir and His Art*, Book Value International (Northbrook, IL: 1981).

Wills, Geoffry, *Practical Guide to Antique Collecting*, Gramercy Publishing, Co. (New York, NY: 1961).

Wilson, Gillian, *Selections from the Decorative Arts in the J. Paul Getty Museum*, The J. Paul Gety Museum (Malibu, CA.: 1983).

Winchester, Alice, edited by and the staff of the *Antiques Magazine*, *The Antiques Book*, Bonanza Books (New York, NY: 1950).

Wintersgill, Donald, *English Antiques: 1700-1830*, William Morrow & Co. (New York, NY: 1975).

Wissinger, Joanna, *Lost & Found: Decorating with Unexpected Objects*, Macmillan Publishing Co. (New York, NY: 1991).

Wood, Elizabeth Davys, *Painting Miniatures*, A&C Black (London: 1989).

Wood, Serry (pseud.), Freeman, Larry, *Haviland-Limoges*, Century House (New York, NY: 1951).

Wright, Veva Penick, *Pamper Your Possessions*, Barre Publishers (Barre, MS: 1972).

Young, Harriet, *Grandmother's Haviland*, Wallace-Homestead Book Co. (Iowa: 1970).

Yoxall, J.H., *Collecting Old Miniatures*, George H. Doran Company (New York, NY: 1916).

# Value Guide

In response to antique dealers I am including a range of prices. As I stated in Chapter 6 prices are variable, so the following serves only as a guide. Secondary market value is determined by many factors.

## Photo Journal (Chapter 2)

### Les Classics

| No. | Price | Description |
|---|---|---|
| 1 | $125-$150 | Square box, pink ribbon |
| 2 | $135-$150 | Rectangular box, pink background |
| 3 | $125-$135 | Oval box, flower bouquet |
| 4 | $140-$160 | Spherical box, floral motif |
| 5 | $125-$135 | Egg-shaped box, floral clusters |
| 6 | $140-$160 | Johnny-jump-up central motif |
| 7 | $165-$175 | Romantic flowered box |
| 8 | $125-$155 | Brass filigree base |
| 9 | $135-$155 | Woven basket base |
| 10 | $250-$300 | Three bottles and funnel in container |
| 11 | $300-$350 | Perfume container w/bottles and funnel |
| 12 | $115-$145 | Lead crystal base |
| 13 | $160-$180 | Basket with blooms central motif |
| 14 | $150-$170 | Blue cornflower motif |
| 15 | $175-$200 | Vibrant yellow background |
| 16 | $125-$150 | Perfume bottle |
| 17 | $125-$150 | Perfume container with gold background |
| 18 | $125-$135 | Napoleonic box |
| 19 | $110-$135 | Raised design heart-shaped box |
| 20 | $140-$160 | Fan-shaped box |
| 21 | $125-$175 | Golden apple box |
| 22 | $125-$150 | Melon fluted box |
| 23 | $125-$150 | Bouquet tied with pink ribbon motif |
| 24 | $125-$150 | Flower festooned covered vessel |
| 25 | $100-$125 | Oval box with rosettes |
| 26 | $110-$135 | Cranberry-pink background on box |
| 27 | $125-$145 | Heart-shaped box with posies |
| 28 | $125-$150 | Bodkin container with musical clasp |
| 29 | $170-$195 | Spherical container with thimble |
| 30 | $135-$150 | Rectangular box with blue blooms and gold stripes |
| 31 | $150-$175 | Egg-shaped box with perfume container |
| 32 | $130-$150 | Oval lily of the valley box |
| 33 | $125-$135 | Crazy paved box |
| 34 | $125-$150 | Snuffbox with spectacles |
| 35 | $135-$150 | Cupid and dove heart-shaped box |
| 36 | $200-$250 | Blue flower bouquet perfume container |
| 37 | $225-$275 | Bird perfume container |
| 38 | $175-$225 | Etui with beautiful woman |
| 39 | $140-$160 | Heart-shaped box with floral garland |
| 40 | $175-$190 | Envelope box with cancelled stamp |
| 41 | $115-$135 | "Remember the giver" box |

### Pour Une Occasion Speciale

| No. | Price | Description |
|---|---|---|
| 42 | $250-$275 | Chilled champagne box |
| 43 | $125-$150 | Heart-shaped box with floral garland |
| 44 | $180-$195 | Two figures kissing box |
| 45 | $125-$150 | "Amour Amour" box |
| 46 | $100-$115 | "I Love You" box |
| 47 | $250-$275 | Bride and groom atop cake box |
| 48 | $200-$225 | "Just Married" limo box |
| 49 | $175-$200 | Birthday cake on plate |
| 50 | $185-$200 | Valentine cherub |
| 51 | $135-$155 | Shamrock center motif |
| 52 | $180-$195 | Duo of rabbits |
| 53 | $200-$220 | Floral envelope |
| 54 | $175-$200 | Graduation-themed box |
| 55 | $145-$165 | Fourth of July flag |
| 56 | $200-$215 | Halloween box with witch |
| 57 | $180-$195 | Thanksgiving cornucopia |
| 58 | $145-$160 | Thanksgiving turkey box |
| 59 | $185-$200 | Indian carrying basket of corn box. |
| 60 | $150-$175 | Chanukah menorah |
| 61 | $175-$200 | Star of David dreidel box |
| 62 | $175-$200 | Christmas tree box |
| 63 | $180-$200 | Christmas cup and saucer with brass spoon clasp |
| 64 | $145-$155 | Holly with tassels box |
| 65 | $200-$225 | Holiday box with Santa on train |
| 66 | $150-$170 | Drum-shaped box |

### Bon Appetit

| No. | Price | Description |
|---|---|---|
| 67 | $165-$185 | Strawberry-topped box |
| 68 | $190-$210 | Charlotte russe topped box |
| 69 | $160-$180 | Peach basket with brass handles |
| 70 | $150-$175 | Fruit basket |
| 71 | $140-$160 | Chef's toque |
| 72 | $150-$175 | Strawberry tart |
| 73 | $110-$130 | Radish with brass bunny |

| No. | Price | Description |
|---|---|---|
| 74 | $185-$200 | Vegetable basket with bee |
| 75 | $175-$195 | Eggplant container |
| 76 | $175-$195 | Avocado box |
| 77 | $100-$125 | Asparagus plate |
| 78 | $175-$200 | Pomegranate box |
| 79 | $275-$350 | Fruit cart with floral basket clasp |
| 80 | $125-$175 | Picnic basket with brass handle |
| 81 | $150-$175 | Artichoke box |
| 82 | $165-$175 | Pea pod with flower clasp |
| 83 | $150-$175 | Cauliflower box |
| 84 | $175-$200 | Domed cheese board |
| 85 | $125-$135 | Gouda and Swiss cheese topped box |
| 86 | $250-$300 | Asst. cheeses topped box |
| 87 | $155-$175 | Wine basket |
| 88 | $250-$300 | Pasta and wine bottle topped box |
| 89 | $175-$200 | Wine serving basket |
| 90 | $165-$185 | Grape basket |
| 91 | $215-$235 | Tureen with vegetable motif |
| 92 | $155-$175 | Green grapes |
| 93 | $155-$175 | Sardine box |
| 94 | $135-$155 | Beluga Caviar |
| 95 | $180-$210 | Salmon platter |
| 96 | $135-$165 | Napoleon on porcelain plate |
| 97 | $175-$200 | Tea caddy container |
| 98 | $140-$160 | Chef's hat box |
| 99 | $135-$155 | Veilleuse with poppy design |
| 100 | $165-$175 | Fresh pears on plate |
| 101 | $235-$265 | Tea set on tray box |
| 102 | $175-$200 | Melon on plate with spoon clasp |
| 103 | $145-$165 | Apple slice box |
| 104 | $175-$195 | Sliced apple on plate |
| 105 | $185-$210 | Compote with array of fruits |
| 106 | $250-$270 | Picnic basket |
| 107 | $185-$210 | Footed fruit bowl |
| 108 | $235-$260 | Breakfast tray |
| 109 | $125-$135 | Profiteroles stack |
| 110 | $155-$165 | Tureen with floral motif |

## Le Jardin

| No. | Price | Description |
|---|---|---|
| 111 | $200-$225 | Hydrangea pot |
| 112 | $220-$240 | Hyacinth pot with perfume vial |
| 113 | $175-$190 | Bunny at arbored gate |
| 114 | $195-$210 | Angel amidst pansies |
| 115 | $215-$230 | Bench with flowers and hat |
| 116 | $135-$145 | Watering can |
| 117 | $175-$200 | Gardening book |
| 118 | $140-$160 | Watering can with fruit basket and green trellising |

| No. | Price | Description |
|---|---|---|
| 119 | $175-$200 | Bouquet of orange anemones |
| 120 | $145-$165 | Ladybug on leaf |
| 121 | $125-$145 | Pansy |
| 122 | $145-$165 | Morning glory |
| 123 | $145-$165 | Rose |
| 124 | $125-$145 | Flower with bee |
| 125 | $125-$145 | Orange poppy |
| 126 | $175-$195 | Heart-shaped box with pair of birds |
| 127 | $135-$145 | Yellow rose bud |
| 128 | $125-$135 | Watering can with brass snail clasp |
| 129 | $135-$145 | Stargazer lily |
| 130 | $165-$185 | Wheelbarrow |
| 131 | $175-$195 | Pot and gardening tools |
| 132 | $115-$125 | Lilies of the valley heart-shaped box |
| 133 | $155-$175 | Watering can with two hand-painted birds |
| 134 | $115-$125 | Skep-shaped box |
| 135 | $110-$125 | Textured walnut |
| 136 | $155-$165 | Acorn with oak leaf |

## Les Animaux

| No. | Price | Description |
|---|---|---|
| 137 | $235-$245 | Boxer with boxing gloves |
| 138 | $175-$185 | Kitten with spilt milk |
| 139 | $190-$210 | Bichon Frise with butterfly |
| 140 | $155-$165 | West Highland Terrier box |
| 141 | $190-$200 | Maltese with grooming items |
| 142 | $195-$210 | Mom and kitten |
| 143 | $200-$225 | Dachshund on barrel-shaped stand |
| 144 | $175-$190 | Cat with fishbowl |
| 145 | $160-$180 | Hen and chicks on nest |
| 146 | $190-$210 | Horse-topped box |
| 147 | $160-$180 | Chicken on fence |
| 148 | $200-$210 | Milkmaid and cow box |
| 149 | $190-$210 | Cat guarding precious goods |
| 150 | $190-$210 | Billy goat with hay |
| 151 | $140-$160 | Frog-topped box |
| 152 | $200-$225 | Oval box with frog and beetle |
| 153 | $160-$175 | Snail box |
| 154 | $200-$220 | Pheasant box |
| 155 | $135-$150 | Sun-basking turtle |
| 156 | $160-$170 | Duo of ducks |
| 157 | $165-$185 | Owl box |
| 158 | $175-$185 | Penguin box |
| 159 | $175-$195 | Birds sharing cherry |
| 160 | $175-$195 | Mother swan box |
| 161 | $260-$280 | Eagle on branch box |
| 162 | $190-$210 | Stout and sturdy ram |
| 163 | $135-$155 | Kangaroo with joey |

| No. | Price | Description |
|-----|-------|-------------|
| 164 | $155-$165 | Koala cub and mom on branch |
| 165 | $155-$165 | Majestic tiger |
| 166 | $220-$240 | Resting camel topped box |
| 167 | $155-$165 | Alligator box, leaf clasp |
| 168 | $190-$210 | Resting fox, bunny clasp |
| 169 | $155-$165 | Rabbit with vegetables |
| 170 | $180-$195 | Alert fox topped box with leaf clasp |
| 171 | $150-$195 | Nut gathering squirrel |
| 172 | $200-$220 | Beaver wearing overalls |
| 173 | $360-$380 | Monkey with peach clasp |
| 174 | $190-$205 | Angel fish in bowl |
| 175 | $150-$195 | Dolphin in surf |
| 176 | $180-$195 | Tropical fish box |

## Pour Les Petits

| No. | Price | Description |
|-----|-------|-------------|
| 177 | $90-$100 | "Baby's Curls" box |
| 178 | $180-$195 | Baby in bassinet |
| 179 | $90-$100 | "First Haircut" box |
| 180 | $245-$260 | Fiddle-playing cat |
| 181 | $200-$215 | Peter Pumpkineater's wife in pumpkin |
| 182 | $215-$235 | Old woman in a shoe |
| 183 | $230-$250 | Teeter-tottering teddies |
| 184 | $260-$290 | Teddy with epaulets |
| 185 | $175-$200 | Bear sleeping in bed |
| 186 | $200-$215 | Umbrella |
| 187 | $280-$300 | Noah's Ark |
| 188 | $150-$195 | Dressed up bunny |
| 189 | $150-$195 | Elegant elephant |
| 190 | $200-$215 | Triple turtle box |
| 191 | $180-$195 | Three mitten-seeking kittens |
| 192 | $105-$120 | Three monkeys on a log |
| 193 | $175-$190 | Dalmatian with basketball |
| 194 | $150-$160 | Ice-cream truck |
| 195 | $170-$190 | Gymnast bear on pommel horse |
| 196 | $155-$175 | Train with bow clasp |
| 197 | $155-$195 | Toy box with teddy bear clasp |
| 198 | $175-$190 | Hand-painted rocking horse |

## En Voyage

| No. | Price | Description |
|-----|-------|-------------|
| 199 | $250-$300 | Six lions with mounted globe |
| 200 | $200-$210 | Eiffel tower |
| 201 | $130-$140 | Well-traveled hat box |
| 202 | $170-$205 | Arc de Triomphe |
| 203 | $310-$325 | Notre Dame Cathedral |
| 204 | $175-$190 | Pyramid atrium from the Louvre |
| 205 | $175-$195 | Sacre Coer with flying angels |
| 206 | $240-$265 | Chateau de Chenonceau with wandering minstrel |

| No. | Price | Description |
|-----|-------|-------------|
| 207 | $210-$230 | Train on multi-dimensional box |
| 208 | $125-$145 | Fleur-de-lys |
| 209 | $225-$235 | Queen chess piece |
| 210 | $160-$180 | Crown |
| 211 | $225-$235 | King chess piece |
| 212 | $180-$200 | Big Ben |
| 213 | $335-$365 | Hinged castle |
| 214 | $190-$210 | Windmill box |
| 215 | $155-$175 | Wooden shoes |
| 216 | $180-$195 | Egyptian pyramid |
| 217 | $180-$190 | Sphinx |
| 218 | $180-$195 | Ancient Egyptian tome |
| 219 | $155-$175 | Sydney Opera House |
| 220 | $175-$190 | Travel journal |
| 221 | $190-$205 | Hut and palm tree |
| 222 | $200-$215 | Traveler with hat |
| 223 | $235-$255 | Beach bag box |
| 224 | $225-$235 | Bathing beauty |
| 225 | $230-$250 | The White House |
| 226 | $190-$205 | Empire State Building |
| 227 | $200-$225 | New York apple with torch clasp |
| 228 | $200-$225 | Lighthouse box |
| 229 | $200-$210 | Golden Gate Bridge |
| 230 | $200-$210 | Pebble Beach golf course |
| 231 | $165-$175 | Hippie Backpack |
| 232 | $200-$225 | Hollywood western box |
| 233 | | Set of Hollywood chair and camera boxes |
| | a) $125-$135 | Chair |
| | b) $150-$165 | Camera |

## Moyens de Transport

| No. | Price | Description |
|-----|-------|-------------|
| 234 | $175-$185 | Venetian gondolier topped box |
| 235 | $175-$185 | Steamship with helm clasp |
| 236 | $165-$185 | Chinese junk |
| 237 | $175-$195 | Sail boat |
| 238 | $235-$250 | Titanic with anchor clasp |
| 239 | $145-$155 | Double bus |
| 240 | $200-$250 | London taxi |
| 241 | $245-$265 | Packard with car clasp |
| 242 | $200-$215 | Pony express stagecoach |
| 243 | $200-$225 | Yellow school bus |
| 244 | $200-$220 | Engine with cow catcher |
| 245 | $175-$195 | Red gas pump |
| 246 | $190-$210 | Motorcycle with boot clasp |
| 247 | $190-$210 | Red dune buggy |
| 248 | $200-$250 | Single propeller plane |
| 249 | $200-$250 | Airport box |
| 250 | $200-$235 | Helicopter |
| 251 | $200-$215 | Rocket on launch pad |

| No. | Price | Description |
|---|---|---|
| 252 | $235-$250 | Space shuttle |
| 253 | $185-$200 | Apollo module |

## Beaux Arts (Fine Arts)

| No. | Price | Description |
|---|---|---|
| 254 | $175-$185 ea. | Monet boxes |
| 255 | $200-$220 | Anthony Hopkins box |
|  | $150-$190 | Barry Manilow box |
| 256 | $190-$210 | Violin and Mozart music |
| 257 | $210-$230 | Lorgnette |
| 258 | $155-$170 | Musical instrument motif on button-shaped box |
| 259 | $165-$180 | Harp |
| 260 | $190-$210 | Violin and carrying case |
| 261 | $275-$295 | Grand piano |
| 262 | $190-$200 | French horn |
| 263 | $170-$180 | Miniature books |
| 264 | $160-$170 | Upright piano |
| 265 | $130-$145 | Artist's palette |
| 266 | $170-$190 | Paint tube |
| 267 | $260-$290 | Harlequin |
| 268 | $125-$135 | Musical theme box |
| 269 | $200-$225 | Easel |
| 270 | $125-$150 | Blue trunk containing perfume bottles |
| 271 | $275-$300 | Frog with bass fiddle |
| 272 | $230-$250 | Fiddling frog with case |
| 273 | $275-$300 | Cello-playing frog |

## Sport De Plein Air

| No. | Price | Description |
|---|---|---|
| 274 | $180-$195 | Lion tennis player |
| 275 | $175-$195 | Racquet box |
| 276 | $175-$190 | Racing rabbit |
| 277 | $200-$225 | Golf-related box with shoes |
| 278 | $145-$160 | Driver and ball |
| 279 | $175-$195 | Golf bag with ball clasp |
| 280 | $175-$190 | Diving frog |
| 281 | $200-$225 | Croquet box |
| 282 | $140-$160 | Woven pattern fishing box |
| 283 | $155-$165 | Hand-painted creel |
| 284 | $260-$275 | Hot air balloon |
| 285 | $175-$185 | Mountaineering |
| 286 | $185-$200 | Skate box with bow clasp |

## La Mode

| No. | Price | Description |
|---|---|---|
| 287 | $175-$190 | Portrait neckline |
| 288 | $160-$170 | Handbag with chain strap and bow clasp |
| 289 | $160-$170 | Hat with pink ribbon and flowers |
| 290 | $190-$210 | Polka-dotted chapeau |
| 291 | $175-$190 | Neckline box |
| 292 | $190-$205 | Bag with latticework |

| No. | Price | Description |
|---|---|---|
| 293 | $275-$300 | Box with shoes |
| 294 | $175-$195 | Leopard skin corseted mannequin |
| 295 | $175-$185 | Leopard skin shoes and box |
| 296 | $140-$160 | Summer hat with flower clasp |
| 297 | $135-$155 | Paris couture mannequin |
| 298 | $160-$170 | Handbag box with bow clasp |
| 299 | $200-$215 | Dress on mannequin |
| 300 | $155-$175 | Hat with roses |
| 301 | $270-$285 | Jewel-buckled shoe |

## Messages

| No. | Price | Description |
|---|---|---|
| 302 | $150-$170 | Crossword puzzle box |
| 303 | $125-$145 | "I Love You" box |
| 304 | $140-$160 | Telephone on skirted table |
| 305 | $140-$150 | Black rotary phone |
| 306 | $140-$160 | Telephone box |
| 307 | $110-$125 | "Le Monde" box |
| 308 | $175-$185 | Pen box |
| 309 | $160-$180 | Declaration of Independence box |
| 310 | $160-$180 | Malachite stamp box |
| 311 | $120-$135 | Pen box |
| 312 | $140-$150 | Inkwell with roses |

## Mobilier Miniature

| No. | Price | Description |
|---|---|---|
| 313 | $225-$250 | Silver fruit bowl on table |
| 314 | $200-$225 | Serving cart |
| 315 | $175-$195 | Mahogany coffee table |
| 316 | $270-$285 | Canopy box |
| 317 | $175-$190 | Tea for two |
| 318 | $175-$190 | Window-topped box |
| 319 | $200-$225 | Writing desk box |
| 320 | $200-$225 | Washstand box |
| 321 | $200-$225 | Vanity table box |
| 322 | $180-$190 | Comfortable chair |
| 323 | $190-$210 | Sabbath table |
| 324 | $250-$275 | Washstand with accessory items |
| 325 | $170-$180 | Armoire with faux mirror |
| 326 | $190-$210 | Skirted table set for intimate dinner |
| 327 | $200-$225 | Couple in bed |

## Merveilles Caches

| No. | Price | Description |
|---|---|---|
| 328 | $250-$275 | Bowed front box |
| 329 | $300-$325 | Champagne house |
| 330 | $190-$220 | Wine crate |
| 331 | $180-$200 | Oyster box |
| 332 | $175-$195 | Garden party |
| 333 | $275-$300 | Gilded bird cage |
| 334 | $180-$225 | Hummingbird inkwell |
| 335 | $255-$275 | Egg box |
| 336 | $275-$325 | Noah's Ark |
| 337 | $230-$250 | Tea house box |

## Miscellaneous Treasures (Chapter 4)

| No. | Price | Description |
| --- | --- | --- |
| 1 | $75-$100 | Covered candy box |
| 2 | $100-$125 | Jewelry casket |
| 3 | $75-$100 | Collar button/stud box |
| 4 | $60-$100 | Powder box w/gold bands |
| 5 | $60-$100 | Powder box w/pink roses |
| 6 | $40-$60 | Pomade container |
| 7 | $50-$80 | Button box |
| 8 | $60-$100 | Power box w/violets |
| 9 | $125-$175 | Accessory box |
| 10 | $60-$100 | Hinged box w/bird |
| 11 | $50-$80 | Hinged box w/fleur-de-lys |
| 12 | $60-$100 | Hinged box w/floral central motif |
| 13 | $65-$125 | Hinged box w/ellipsoid shape |
| 14 | $60-$100 | Hinged box w/bee and olive wreath |
| 15 | $125-$175 | Bonbonniere w/reclining woman |
| 16 | $125-$175 | Bonbonniere w/lizard |
| 17 | $125-$175 | Hinged box bas relief of two fish |
| 18 | $100-$115 | Bonbonniere of cat |
| 19 | $75-$100 | Conserve container |
| 20 | $50-$75 | Hair receiver w/flowers |
| 21 | $300-$350 | Tobacco jar |
| 22 | $60-$100 | Sugar holder |
| 23 | $65-$100 | Marabout with gilded handle |
| 24 | $25-$45 | Covered butter |
| 25 | $125-$175 | Chocolate pot |
| 26 | $125-$150 | Mustard pot |
| 27 | $100-$125 | Porringer |
| 28 | $175-$225 | Sauceboat |
| 29 | $25-$35 | Salt cellar |
| 30 | $50-$90 | Cigarette container |
| 31 | $125-$175 | Covered bonbon box w/cherub medallion |
| 32 | $150-$225 | Covered bonbon box w/roses |
| 33 | $50-$60 | Covered bonbon w/art nouveau-style design |
| 34 | $50-$75 | Puff box |
| 35 | $100-$150 | Hair receiver and puff box |
| 36 | $155-$175 | Dresser set |
| 37 | $50-$75 | Sardine box |
| 38 | $195-$295 | Tobacco jar |
| 39 | $60-$100 | Dresser box w/roses |
| 40 | $75-$110 | Powder box |
| 41 | $90-$120 | Dresser box and hair receiver |
| 42 | $125-$175 | Bonbonniere of orange cat |
| 43 | $125-$175 | Bonbonniere of curled cat |
| 44 | $100-$125 | Oval hinged box |
| 45 | $125-$175 | Hinged box with cats in basket |
| 46 | $600-$700 | Hinged box w/couple |